QUEEN
OF THE
UNDERWORLD

SOPHIE
LYONS

EDITED BY MATTHEW WHITLEY

Queen of the Underworld
Sophie Lyons, 2013

ISBN-13: 978-1-938660-09-2

Originally published under the title *Why Crime Does Not Pay* by J. S. Ogilvie Publishing Co. in 1913.

This edition published by Combustion Books:
www.combustionbooks.org
info@combustionbooks.org

fonts used:
Adobe Garamond Pro
Tw Cen
LAUDANUM

CONTENTS

Rogue's Gallery

Welcome to the Rogue's Gallery. With this series, we showcase amazing lives lived regardless of law and so many of the conventions of society. We will be reprinting out-of-print works, like this book you hold in your hands, as well as bringing out new titles of adventurous lives.

In this, our first release, we bring you Sophie Lyon's 1913 memoir, originally and ironically titled *Why Crime Does Not Pay*. It was the style at the time to release these lurid and truthful descriptions of the joys of the criminal life under titles that denounced the crimes within—over and over in this book, the author repeats that crime doesn't pay. Yet as we can see by Sophie Lyon's example, it most certainly can. In 1913, then in her mid-60s, she retired from crime with a fortune of half a million dollars and more than forty houses to her name, owing to her wise investment of the loot she gathered from swindles, shoplifting, and bank robbery. This fortune she set to the singular task of aiding criminals and their families during times of incarceration, offering free rent to criminals under the guise of philanthropy.

Sophie Lyons was born a pauper and yet refused to live as a pauper ought. She wanted the finer things in life, so she took them, and she retired as rich as she could hope.

EDITOR'S INTRODUCTION

QUEEN OF THE UNDERWORLD

A "THIEF FROM THE CRADLE," IN THE WORDS OF ONE POLICE CAP-tain—Sophie Lyons' initiation into the New York City underworld was a matter of birthright. By the age of three she had already claimed her inheritance and assumed her mother's place as a success-ful working pickpocket. Her virtuosity aside, Lyons was no curiosity, but was only one of many in a 19th-century brood of hustlers, con men, and thieves that had been systematically barred from "healthy" institutions and quarantined in slums or prisons. This underclass had few options but to take by force what wealth they had been denied.

The result of this was a garishness that defied their hygienic separa-tion: a vibrant silk scarf worn on a rough neck. The era's rogues' galleries attest to this, showing thieves still dripping with the luxury of their robberies, as if playing the part of a successful industrialist. You should not be taken in by the dissonance of this image, however. These were a people of an innately different logic—routinely committing the great American sin of letting their wealth idle and waste, oftentimes burning through more than one fortune in their flamboyant lives. Unlike the commerce-driven criminals who still make their home in the shadowed palm of the hand of the marketplace, such as the Italian Mafia and

Japanese Yakuza, Sophie Lyons and those like her were below and to the left, in a social wound.

"I don't belong to the working class. I belong to the criminal classes."

This wound, although unorganized, seeded the germ of an alien language—the delirious slang of thieves' flash stitched together from many national roots, an alien morality, and a surprisingly well-networked way of life. It rejected work as both a necessity and as a Marxist virtue, refusing the gilding of their tears. The product of all this was a monstrosity that treasured luxury and yet despoiled it just as quickly. A monstrosity that, while not charitable, was loyal to itself and dignified, as Lyons shows us through fur-coat-clad prison breaks and a suicidal gamble to leverage an infamous portrait against bourgeois vanity to secure a fellow thief's release.

The underworld that she sketched and inhabited was dominated by lifestyles impossible to assimilate and most concerned with the rush of the hunt. It was a world that is plainly seductive, with its collection of costume jewelry brigands, all hand painted, and beautifully mutinous, standing against a backdrop of silver halide.

And yet in her memoir, Lyons offers a routine lament, that it was all for naught and was a fool's mission, in a crude attempt to plaster over the glaring antagonism that is still visible in her story. We ask you to forgive her.

In Lyons' time, there was a little-celebrated racetrack scam known as horse ringing. Theatre makeup artists would turn their hand from the next Shakespearean death mask to disguising prize-winning horses as broken hags. Champions would be paraded with their haunches awkwardly bulging, their eyes yellowed, and their faces daubed with the slack-jawed pigment of a has-been. Suddenly, race favorites were listed as 20-to-1 long shots. The bookmakers and our beauty school hoodlums placed bets on their lame horses and walked away rich.

A similar sleight of hand was performed by the publishers of the day, bending their more antisocial subjects into digestible poses for mass appeal and legal protection. Famous criminal biographies of the era, Jack Black's *You Can't Win*, George White's *The Penalty and Redemption*, and here Lyons' autobiography originally released under the title *Crime Doesn't Pay* all bear the signs—

> a calligraphic motion of the cross & a lipstick frown
> lead rabbit ears affixed to keep the neck at a servile 12 degrees

Sophie's insistence on the futility of the outlaw life is the most uncomfortable trace of this deception. And so we've put the dead to work for the living. As an act of perfect cowardice, we've rubbed out the original publication's sanitized veneer long after its subject could resist. Re-dressed and trimmed of its moral simplicity, we offer our own restoration more fittingly titled *Queen of the Underworld*. We find the colors to be more rich without the gray wash of a cost-benefit analysis. Against these empty frames Sophie Lyons' underclass collage flickers with the proper power:

> razors exploring slits in velvet purses,
> folds of silk overlaid against constellations of lead shot scars,
> world-renowned canvases cut, frayed & secreted
> > to be perfumed w/ fear heavy sweat.

CHAPTER I

HOW I BEGAN MY CAREER OF CRIME

I WAS NOT QUITE SIX YEARS OLD WHEN I STOLE MY FIRST POCKETBOOK. I was very happy because I was petted and rewarded; my wretched stepmother patted my curly head, gave me a bag of candy, and said I was a "good girl."

My stepmother was a thief. My good father never knew this. He went to the war at President Lincoln's call for troops and left me with his second wife, my stepmother.

Scarcely had my father's regiment left New York than my stepmother began to busy herself with my education—not for a useful career, but for a career of crime. Patiently she instructed me, beginning with the very rudiments of thieving—how to help myself to things that lay unprotected in candy shops, drug stores, and grocery stores. I was made to practice at home until my childish fingers had acquired considerable dexterity.

Finally, I was told that money was the really valuable thing to possess, and that the successful men and women were those who could take pocketbooks. With my stepmother as the model to practice on I was taught how to open shopping bags, feel out the loose money or the pocketbook, and get it into my little hands without attracting the attention of my victims. In those days leather bags were not common—most women carried cloth or knitted shopping bags. I was provided with a very sharp little knife and was carefully instructed how to slit open the bags so that I could get my fingers in.

And at last, when I had arrived at a sufficient degree of proficiency, I was taken out by my stepmother and we traveled over into New York's shopping district. I was sent into a store and soon came out with a pocketbook—my stepmother petted me and rewarded me.

ARRESTED FOR PICKING POCKETS

That was the beginning of my career as a professional criminal. I did not know it was wrong to steal; nobody ever taught me that. What I was told was wrong, and what I was punished for, was when I came home with only one pocketbook instead of many.

All during my early childhood I did little but steal, and was never sent to school. I did not learn to read or write until I was twenty-five years old. If my stepmother brought me to a place where many persons congregated and I was slow in getting pocketbooks and other articles, she would stick a pin into my arm to remind me that I must be more industrious. If a pin was not convenient she would step on my toes or pinch me when occasion made her think I was in need of some such stimulant.

One time we went over to Hoboken to a place where a merry-go-round was operating, and my stepmother sent me into the crowds to take pocketbooks and anything else I could put my hands on. A detective saw me take a woman's pocketbook and he carried me off to jail in his arms, my stepmother disappearing in the crowd. I remained in the Hoboken jail several days and was very happy there, for the policemen used to give me candy and let me play around the place, and did not beat me, as my stepmother used to do. A strange woman came and took me home, for my absence was felt because of the loss of the money I used to bring home every night. I was arrested very often when a small girl, but usually got out after a few days, as my stepmother knew how to bring influence to bear in my favor. One time I was sent to Randall's Island and used to play with the daughters of the assistant superintendent, whose name was Jones. The little girls learned from their father that I was a thief, and they used to sympathize with me and make things pleasant, knowing that it was not my fault, but the fault of my stepmother, who forced me to do wrong.

A THIEF FROM THE CRADLE

I did most of my stealing when a little girl by putting my hands into men's and women's pockets, but I also used to cut a hole in the bags carried by women—and then insert my fingers and take out the money or other things I found there, as I have already mentioned. Hardly a day passed when I did not steal a considerable sum of money, and many days I would take home more than a hundred dollars. Sometimes I would forget my work and be attracted to a store window and buy a doll for myself to pet. When I went home to my house and sat down on the steps to cuddle my doll my stepmother or my brother would come out and catch me up and give me a good many hard knocks for neglecting my duty—and the only duty I knew in those days was to steal, and never stop stealing.

More than once when I would dread going home I would have myself arrested by stealing so a policeman could see me do it. But it didn't help me much, for my stepmother never failed to get me out of jail within a few days after my arrest. It seemed so natural for me to steal that one time when I was arrested the policeman asked me what I was doing, and I said frankly, "Picking pockets." He asked me how many I got, and I said, "I don't know; I gave them all to my momma."

Every day I would wear a different kind of dress so as not to attract attention, in case anybody who saw me steal something the day before happened to be around. My stepmother was wise enough to disguise me in this way, and it enabled me to keep working for a long time in the same place. My stepmother would take me into the department stores and wait outside for me. If I came out with enough money to satisfy her she would say nothing, but march me off home or to another store for more money, but if I came out with less than she expected, then I would get the pin pricks or pinches, and be made to feel that I had done something wrong in not working harder and stealing more.

I was, indeed, as one chief of police once said, "A thief from the cradle." Surrounding my childhood and youth there was not one wholesome or worthy influence. My friends and companions were always criminals, and it is not surprising that in my early womanhood I should have fallen in love with a bank burglar—Ned Lyons.

Following this romance came motherhood and an awakening within me of at least one worthy resolve—that, whatever had been my career, I certainly would see that my children were given the benefit of a tender mother's love, which I had never had, and that my little ones should be surrounded with every pure and wholesome influence.

The first few years of my married life were divided between my little ones and the necessary exactions which my career imposed on me. Ned Lyons, my husband, was a member of the boldest and busiest group of bank robbers in the world. Here and there, all over the Eastern States, we went on expeditions, forcing the vaults of the biggest and richest banks in the country. We had money in plenty, but we spent money foolishly. When we crept out of the vaults of the great Manhattan Bank in the early morning hours of the night of that famous robbery, we had nearly $3,000,000 in money, bonds, and securities. And from the Northampton Bank we took $200,000, if I remember correctly.

But we had our troubles. My husband, Ned Lyons, was a desperate scoundrel, and was constantly in difficulties. My desire was to be with my little ones, but the gang of burglars with whom I was associated had learned to make me useful, and they insisted on my accompanying them on their expeditions. I will explain fully in following chapters just what my part was in many of their various exploits.

Ned Lyons was hungry for money—money, more money—and the desperate risks he took and his continual activity took me away from the children much of the time.

MY ESCAPE FROM SING SING

Always there was something going on, and I had very little peace. Early one winter Ned Lyons, in connection with Jimmy Hope, George Bliss, Ira Kingsland, and others, blew open the safe of the Waterford,

New York Bank and secured $150,000. Lyons and two others were caught, convicted and sent to Sing Sing Prison.

It was not long before I myself was captured, convicted and also sent to Sing Sing for five years. But my husband managed to escape from the prison one December afternoon, and he lost no time in arranging for my escape from the women's section of the prison, which was a separate building just across the road from the main prison.

I was all ready, of course, and when my husband drove up in a sleigh, wonderfully well disguised, wearing a handsome fur coat, and carrying a woman's fur coat on his arm, I made my escape and joined him. I will tell the details of how my husband and I got out of Sing Sing in a subsequent article.

We both went into hiding and made our way to Canada, where Ned, being short of funds, broke into a pawnbroker's safe and helped himself to $20,000 in money and diamonds. With these funds in our pockets we returned to New York, and I kept in hiding as well as I could until my husband, with George Mason and others, robbed the bank at Wellsboro, Pennsylvania. Shortly afterward my husband was arrested while engaged on a job at Riverhead, L.I., and $13,000 worth of railroad bonds were taken from his pockets.

My husband could not let drink alone, and one day he had a street fight with the notorious Jimmy Haggerty, a burglar, who was afterward killed by "Reddy the Blacksmith" in a saloon fight on Houston Street and Broadway. During the fight between Haggerty and Ned Lyons Haggerty managed to bite off the greater portion of my husband's left ear. This was a great misfortune to him as it served as a means of identification ever after. On another occasion, in a drunken dispute, Ned Lyons was shot at the Star and Garter saloon on Sixth Avenue by "Ham" Brock, a Boston character, who fired two shots, one striking Lyons in the jaw and the other in the body.

My husband soon had the bad luck to be caught in the act of breaking into a jewelry store in South Windham, Conn. As soon as he knew he was discovered, my husband tried to make his escape, and the police shot him as he ran, putting one bullet hole through his body and imbedding another ball in his back.

He was also caught in the burglary of a post-office at Palmer, Massachusetts, where they took the safe out of the store, carried it a short distance out of the village, broke it open, and took the valuables. As I have already said, the men had found me very helpful and insisted on my accompanying them on most of their expeditions. Always, if an arrest was made, I was relied upon to get them out of trouble. This took time, money, and resourcefulness, and kept me away from my little ones against my will.

During this time my children were approaching an age when it would no longer do to have them in our home. Our unexplained absences, our midnight departures, our hurried return in the early morning hours with masks, burglars' tools, and satchels full of stolen valuables would arouse curiosity in their little minds. One thing I had sworn to do—to safeguard my little ones from such wretched influences as had surrounded my childhood. With this in view I sent my little boy and my little girl to schools where I felt sure of kind treatment and a religious atmosphere. And I paid handsomely to make sure that they would receive every care and consideration.

I SEE WHY CRIME DOES NOT PAY

I had scarcely gotten the children well placed in excellent schools in Canada when my husband was caught in one of his robberies. I busied myself with lawyers and spent all the money we had on hand, to no avail, and he was given a long prison sentence. Just at this unfortunate moment I was myself arrested in New York and given a six months' term of imprisonment.

On my account I did not care—but what would become of my children? My sources of income had been brought to a sudden stop. I had no money to send to pay my children's expenses. Then, for the first time, I felt the full horror of a criminal's life. I resolved for my children's sake to find a way to support them honestly. I realized the full truth that crime does not pay.

As I went on day after day serving my term in prison my thoughts were always about my little ones. The frightful recollections of my own childhood had developed in me an abnormal mother love. At last I resolved to write to the institutions where my boy and girl were located and explain that I was unavoidably detained and out of funds, but promising to generously repay them for continuing to care for my children.

But I was too late. The newspapers had printed an account of my arrest, and when it reached the ears of the convent and college authorities where my boy and girl were stopping it filled them with indignation to think that a professional thief had the audacity to place her children under their care. So they immediately took steps to get rid of the innocent youngsters, in spite of the fact that I had paid far in advance for their board and tuition. The boy was shipped off in haste to the poorhouse, and my dear little girl was sent to a public orphanage, from which she was adopted by a man named Doyle, who was a customs inspector in Canada at the time.

When my six months were up my first thoughts were of my children, and I started off to visit them, thinking, of course, that they were still in the institutions where I had placed them. I called at the convent, and when they saw me coming one of the sisters locked the door in my face. I was astounded at this, but determined to know what it meant. As my repeated knocks did not open the door, I resorted to a more drastic method and began to kick on the panels quite vigorously. The inmates of the convent became alarmed at my persistence and feared that the door would be broken open, so they thought it best to open and let me in. I then demanded to know the cause of their peculiar conduct, and one of them spoke up, saying:

"You are a thief, and we do not want you here."

"Oh, is that it?" I replied. "Well, where is my little girl? I want to see her."

"Your child has been placed in a respectable family, and you will not be permitted to see her," answered the sister.

Then my blood began to boil with fury, and I demanded to know why they had sent my girl away without letting me know, especially as I had given them considerable money, and they knew all her expenses would be paid. But she refused to give me any satisfaction. In desperation I sprang at her. She screamed and called for help. The mother superior then made her appearance and, dismayed at the sight of the determination I had displayed, she reluctantly gave me the address of the man who had my little girl.

I did not have a dollar with me at the time, but started off to walk to Mr. Doyle's house, which was some distance in the country. After a few hours' walking I met a man driving by in a buggy, and he stopped and offered me a ride. I, of course, accepted his invitation and got into the buggy. He asked me where I was going, and I said I was searching for a man named Doyle. He wanted my name and the nature of my business, but I said that information would be given to Mr. Doyle himself, and nobody else. He then said his name was Doyle, and asked me my name, and I told him I was Sophie Lyons. As soon as he heard this he stopped the horse and ordered me out of the buggy, and shouted: "You are a very bad woman. I have your little girl. I'm going to keep her. You are not a fit mother, and should be kept in jail, where you belong."

FOR MY CHILDREN'S SAKE

"We will not discuss that here," I replied, "What I want now is to see my little girl, and I wish you would drive me to your house."

"You shall never see your child, and you had better not come near my house," he cried as he whipped up his horse and was soon out of sight, leaving me alone on the road.

I continued my walk, however, and shortly afterward reached the Doyle house and stood outside the gate, while Doyle, with his two sons and two hired men and a dog, watched me from the piazza. I stood there a few moments, and then Doyle came out and asked me what I was doing there, and demanded that I leave the neighborhood at once. He said: "This is my home, and you must go away."

"It may be your home, Mr. Doyle," I answered, "but my child is in there, and I am going to wait here until I see her."

"I have adopted your girl," he said, "and she will be better off here than with you."

"It takes two to make a bargain," I said, "and you did not get my consent when you adopted the girl."

Realizing that it was useless to try to persuade me, he went inside and left me at the gate, where I stood waiting developments. After another long wait Doyle came out again and said:

"Are you still there? What do you want! You know very well it is better for the girl that she remain with us, and not with a thief like you. I will take good care of her, but you shall not see her."

"I know my rights," I replied, "and I will hire a lawyer and compel the convent authorities to show me their books and explain what they have done with the thousands of dollars I left with them to care for my girl. I will make it hot for you and for them before I finish."

This threat must have frightened him a little, for he then asked me if I had had anything to eat that day, and I told him I had not. Then he invited me into the house to get some food, and said he would hitch up the buggy and drive me back to town. I said:

A MOTHER'S LOVE WINS AT LAST

"No, you will not drive me back to town. I will not go back without my girl."

"Now, be reasonable, Mrs. Lyons," he said. "Your little girl is happy here, and she does not like you because you are a bad woman."

"Well," I answered, "if she does not like her mother then you have made her feel that way; you have taught her to dislike me."

After a little more parleying he went into the house and sent out my little girl to talk to me.

"My darling," I said, "don't you want to kiss your own mother?"

"No," she said; "I do not like you, because you are a thief. You are not my mother at all."

My eyes filled with tears at this, and with sobs in my voice I asked her if she did not remember the little prayers I had taught her and the many happy hours we had spent together. The little dear said:

"Yes, I remember the prayers, but I do not want to see you. You are a thief! Go away, please!"

Those words cut me to the heart—from my own precious daughter. And again I was made to realize that crime does not pay!

I lost no time in setting matters in motion which very soon brought back to my arms my daughter. Meanwhile I hastened to the academy where my little boy had been left and demanded to see him. When my boy was brought out to me he was in a disgraceful condition, he seemed to have been utterly neglected, his clothing was ragged and his face as dirty as a chimney sweep's. I was shocked at this and demanded an explanation from the professor who had charge of the institution. He turned on me angrily, and said:

"You have an amazing assurance to place your good-for-nothing brat among honest children. How dare you give us an assumed name and impose on us in this manner? Get your brat out of here at once, for if honest parents knew your character they would take their children out of the school without delay."

"A false name, is it?" I said to the proud professor. "What name did you give when you were caught in a disreputable house?"

This remark startled him. He changed his manner at once and implored me to speak lower and not let anybody know what I said. I had recognized this professor as a man who had visited Detroit a year or so before and had been caught in a disreputable resort by the police on one of their raids. The professor, of course, did not imagine that anybody in Detroit had known him, and so he thought it perfectly safe to assume the role of superior virtue. He apologized for his neglect of my child and begged me to forget the abuse he had heaped upon me. I congratulated myself that the child had not heard his remarks to me, and I departed with my boy.

But my joy over the fact that my little one had not had his mother's wickedness revealed to him was of short duration. I had brought the child to Detroit, where I had begun preparations to make a permanent home, honestly, I hoped. Several persons there owed me money, and among them a barber I had befriended. I tried persistently to get from him what he owed me, but without success.

When I returned home after a little trip I was compelled to make to New York, my boy came up to me, crying, and said:

"Mamma, I don't want to live around here anymore."

I wondered what could have caused the poor boy to speak that way, so I patted him on the back and said:

"Why, what is the matter, dearie? Don't you like this street anymore?"

"Mamma," he sobbed, "I heard something about you which makes me feel awful bad, but I know it isn't true, is it, mamma?"

"Tell me, child, what is it?"

"Well," he answered, "Mr. Wilson, the barber, asked me the day after you left to go downtown on a trip with him, and I went along. He took me into a large building which I heard was the police station. He asked a man to let him see some pictures, and when he got the pictures he showed me one of them which he said was you; and he said you were a thief and the police had to keep your picture so they could find you when you stole things," and then the boy began to sob as if his poor heart would break.

The man had taken my boy down to the police station and had shown him my picture in the rogues' gallery. And again the realization was forced in on me by the reproachful gaze of my boy that crime does not pay.

For a time I managed to get along fairly well and was able by honest efforts to have a little home and to have my children with me. But my old career came up to haunt me and many refused to have business dealings with me when they were informed of my earlier life. At last I was at the end of my resources—should I lose my little home and my children, or should I go back once more, just once more to my old life?

The struggle between my two impulses was finally settled by a visit from two of my old acquaintances of the underworld—Tom Bigelow and Johnny Meaney. They came to ask my help in a promising job which they felt sure would be a success if they could enlist my services—there would be at least $50,000 for me, they said.

"Big Tom" Bigelow was an old-time professional bank burglar, who had learned his business under such leaders as Jimmy Hope and Langdon W. Moore—men who had never found any bank or any vault too much for their skill. Little Johnny Meaney was one of the cleverest "bank sneaks" that ever lived. He would perform the most amazing feats in getting behind bank counters and walking off with large bundles of money. He was so quick and noiseless in his work that he would never have been arrested but for his fondness for women and drink. When under the influence of champagne he would confide in some strange woman he had met only a few days before, and in order to get the reward some of the women would tell the police where to find Johnny.

He had granulated eyelids, and his inflamed eyes were so conspicuous that he could always be recognized easily. He was married and had several children. His wife never knew the kind of work he did. He had a quarrelsome temper, and always got into some dispute with every woman he met, and usually left them feeling unfavorably disposed toward him. Many of the girls who betrayed him did so more through resentment than anything else. I mention these things to show how personal peculiarities and temperament are often serious menaces to criminals. Meaney's specialty was day work. He would walk into a bank during business hours and sneak behind the counter and pick up everything he could lay his hands on. He never did any night work, and knew nothing about safe blowing. As a rule, a man who makes a specialty of night work, with dark lantern, mask, and jimmy, will not attempt any sneak work, and the first-class sneak will not undertake night work. The night robber is guided by the moon, and oftentimes a job will be called off because the cracksmen think the moon is not right for the work. The darker the night the better. But the bank sneak prefers daylight of the brightest kind. He often works right under the eyes of a room full of clerks, and the bigger the crowd in the streets the easier for him to make his escape and lose himself among them.

HOW I PLANNED A BANK ROBBERY

It was a "bank sneak" job they had in mind. The bank was in a small New Jersey city, near enough to New York so that we could lose ourselves in our old haunts on the East Side before the detectives should get hot on our trail.

I went to the town in advance of the other members of the party and rented a small cottage, posing as a widow who planned to settle down there and live on the income of her husband's insurance money.

Soon after setting in my new quarters, I visited the bank and opened a small account. I found the cashier a man who fitted in perfectly with our dishonest designs. He must have been nearly seventy years old and he could not hear or see so well as he should for the security of the funds in his charge.

I saw right away that he was very susceptible to pretty women and was quite willing to drop his work at any time for a half hour's chat with such a comely widow as I looked to be. My task was to look the ground over, find out where the cash was kept, and how and when access to it could best be secured. It was the simplest thing in the world to get these facts after I had worked my way into the cashier's good graces.

I quickly saw that the most favorable time for the robbery was between the hours of 12 and 1 o'clock, when the other two men in the bank went to their homes for lunch, leaving the institution in the charge of the old cashier. At that time the door of the vault was open, and the bundles of currency and securities lay there in full view, ready for us to take away.

It would be an easy matter for Johnny Meaney, who was a small, wiry fellow, light and quiet on his feet as a cat, to slip in through a side entrance while I held the cashier's attention with one of my harmless flirtations and gain access to the vault through the door in the wire cage, which was almost invariably left unlocked. Even if it should be locked on the day we set for the robbery, it would be a simple matter for Johnny to get inside with the aid of one of his skeleton keys.

Accordingly I sent word to my two comrades that the coast was clear and to come on at once. They arrived in due time and, after looking the ground over, confirmed my own judgment that the robbery was an easy one and could be carried out with little risk according to the plan I had made.

The following Tuesday was the day set, because on that day, as I had found out, the bank generally had a large amount of cash on hand. The time fixed was between 12 and 12:30 o'clock, when the assistant cashier, the bookkeeper, and practically all the rest of the town were at their noonday meal.

Everything was definitely settled unless my visit to the bank on Monday should reveal some unlooked for hitch.

The cashier had become thoroughly accustomed to the "pretty widow's" habit of dropping in on him every day at the noon hour, and he was exceedingly glad to see me when I entered as usual, Monday, and began a series of questions about some fictitious investments of mine in the West. Alas! how well I remember how that vain old man enjoyed his innocent flirtation, little suspecting that the object of his regard was there only to make sure that nothing had happened to disarrange the plans for tomorrow's robbery.

WHAT DELAYED OUR PLANS

Luckily for me the bookkeeper was just starting for lunch when I took my accustomed place outside the cashier's window. I had seen the door through which he had to pass to get from inside the wire cage to the outer part of the bank opened and shut a hundred times; and I had always noted with satisfaction not only that it was seldom locked but also that its hinges never gave even the slightest squeak.

But at this moment a most unexpected thing happened.

As the bookkeeper turned the knob of the wire screen door and opened it, a most unearthly scream came from the iron hinges.

The clerk passed on, and the door lazily swung back behind him with another piercing screech that filled me with dismay.

No watchdog could have sounded a more certain alarm than those hinges. My heart sank as I realized how impossible it would be for Johnny Meaney to pass in and out of that creaking door without detection. Bringing my conversation to a hurried close, I went to tell my comrades how our hopes had been dashed by the unexpected development of a squeak in those bothersome hinges.

The difficulty seemed insurmountable until Johnny Meaney, always a quick-witted, resourceful thief, showed us a way out. His suggestion was that the robbery be postponed for a week and that in the meantime we call in the aid of another well-known bank sneak named Bill Taylor to fix those refractory hinges.

This seemed the only possible solution of the problem, as that squeaking had to be stopped, and it was not safe for either of my companions to attempt it. Accordingly, Meaney went back to New York to make the necessary arrangements, and a few days later Taylor appeared on the scene as the suave, well-dressed representative of the company which had built the vault for this bank.

On presentation of his neatly engraved card, Taylor was readily given permission to inspect the vault. During the afternoon he spent in the bank he called attention to the squeaky hinges and suggested that he apply to them some very excellent machine oil he had with him. This he did and the door moved as noiselessly as before.

And incidentally, while Taylor was masquerading as the traveling agent of the safe company and had the freedom of the bank that afternoon he took occasion to fit a key to the wire door. Not that Johnny Meaney could not attend to this himself in case he found the door locked, but Taylor thought he might as well make everything as smooth as possible for Meaney.

Everything was now in shape, and we decided to rob the bank the next day. Just at noon, as the big clock on the Municipal Building was striking 12, I came up the steps of the bank and greeted the old cashier with my customary smile. The bookkeeper and the four other clerks were passing out of the side door to their lunch. Suddenly I spilled out of my hand right in front of the cashier a handful of large coins in such a way that two silver dollars rolled past him and dropped on the floor inside the wire cage. As he laboriously stooped to pick them up I strained my neck and eyes to examine quickly everything inside the cage to make sure that all the bank clerks had gone out—that nobody remained behind the wire railing except the aged cashier.

Moving over as far as possible to one side of the cashier's window, I drew the old cashier's attention to a photograph of a little child in a locket. This brought the back of his head toward the side door of the bank. As he leaned his face down to see it more closely I caught a glimpse out of the corner of my eye of the shadow-like form of Johnny Meaney.

Noiselessly he had come in through the side door. Like a cat he crept to the wire door. With my ears strained for the faintest alarm from those treacherous hinges, I listened as I kept up a rapid fire conversation to hold the attention of the aged cashier.

The wire door swung open noiselessly; Meaney was crouching low; I had lost my view of him as he crept toward the big open door of the bank vault.

On the sidewalk, pacing slowly up and down in front of the side door, was "Big Tom" Bigelow. He was the "outside man" of the job and, although I could not see him, I knew he was on the alert to intercept anybody who might happen in. With some excuse he must stop any clerk who tried to enter through the side door—I myself must intercept any clerk who might chance to return from lunch and enter by the front entrance.

WE GET OUR PLUNDER

With increasing vivaciousness, I rattled along entertaining the cashier. In a few moments I saw the wire door gently open as if by a spirit hand. Creeping low along the floor, a shadow crossed the little corridor to the outside door; noiselessly it opened and closed—the work was done!

And thus this job, which had taken us weeks to plan, was done in less than five minutes from the time I entered the bank until Meaney stole out of a back door with his satchel full of bank notes and securities. Then the three of us quickly made our way by separate routes to New York.

The loss was not discovered until it came time to close the vault for the day, and we thus had nearly three hours' start of the police. A large reward was offered and numerous detectives engaged, but no one was ever arrested for this crime. I am just vain enough to think that the old cashier was probably very reluctant to believe his pretty widow had a share in the robbery, in spite of her mysterious disappearance on the very day it occurred.

Our plunder amounted to $150,000, of which $20,000 was cash and the rest good negotiable bonds. The money was divided and I undertook the marketing of the securities, which were finally disposed of through various channels for $78,000, or about 60 percent, of their value.

Those squeaky door hinges cost Meaney, Bigelow, and myself about $6,000 apiece, for through the addition of Taylor to our party we had to divide the spoils among four persons instead of three. After paying my expenses, my share of these ill-gotten gains amounted to about $20,000. This I thought ample to provide for the wants of my children until I could establish myself in some honorable business, and I returned to Detroit fully determined never again to risk, as I had, a long prison term.

But my good resolutions were short-lived. Two weeks later word came that my husband was in jail for complicity in an attempted bank robbery which had been nipped in the bud and urgently needed my assistance. It took several thousand dollars of the money for which I had paid so dear to secure his liberty and the remainder soon melted away before the numerous needs of my little brood and my husband's unfortunate gambling propensities.

Here I was again just where I was before the robbery of that New Jersey bank. My money was gone, my old reputation still pursued me, nobody would trust me; "once a thief, always a thief" they said; nobody believed in my sincere desire to abandon my early career and lead an honest life.

I did not feel vindictive at the sneers at my protestations of a desire to earn an honest living—I could not blame anybody for doubting my sincerity. But my home and my little ones, dearer to me than life, what was to become of them? Was there no way to escape from my wretched career? If ever a woman and a mother realized that crime does not pay, I was made to learn that truth.

It is a long and difficult road—the narrow path that leads from crime to honest living. I have traveled it, thank heaven! but it was hard, it was slow—and many times I strayed from the path.

Some of my companions of the old days traveled that road with me. A few, a very few, succeeded as I did at last. Many gave it up, turned back. A thousand episodes of my career and of their misguided lives all illuminate the one great inevitable fact that crime does not pay!

CHAPTER II

THE SECRET OF THE STOLEN GAINSBOROUGH—AND THE LESSON OF THE CAREER OF RAYMOND, THE "PRINCE OF SAFE BLOWERS" WHO BUILT A MILLIONAIRE'S RESIDENCE IN A FASHIONABLE LONDON SUBURB AND KEPT A YACHT WITH A CREW OF 20 MEN IN THE MEDITERRANEAN

IT WAS ON THE MORNING OF MAY 15, SEVERAL YEARS AGO, THAT THE manager of Agnew's great art gallery in London turned the key in the lock of the private gallery to show an art patron the famous "Gainsborough." His amiable smile faded from his lips as he came face to face with an empty gilt frame.

The great $125,000 painting had been cut from its frame.

Who stole this masterpiece? How was it stolen? Could it be recovered?

The best detectives of Europe and America were asked to find answers to these questions. They never did. I will answer them here for the first time today.

The man who cut the Gainsborough from its frame was a millionaire, he was an associate of mine, he was a bank burglar. Adam Worth, or Harry Raymond, as he was known to his friends, did not need the money and he did not want the painting—he entered that London art gallery at 3 o'clock in the morning and took that roll of canvas out under his arm for a purpose that nobody suspected. I will explain all this presently.

I have said that Raymond was a millionaire, and I said in previous chapters that crime does not pay—how is it possible to reconcile these two statements? We shall see.

Among all my old acquaintances and associates in the criminal world, perhaps no one serves better as an example of the truth that crime does not pay than this very millionaire burglar, this man who had earned the title of the "Prince of Safe Blowers." For a time he seemed to have everything his heart could desire—a mansion, servants, liveried equipages, a yacht; and it all crumbled away like a house of cards, vanished like the wealth of Aladdin in the Arabian Nights. And so Raymond, most "successful" bank robber of the day, lived to learn the lesson that crime does not pay.

Raymond was a Massachusetts boy—bright, wide awake, but headstrong. Born of an excellent family and well educated, he formed bad habits and developed a passion for gambling.

RAYMOND'S FIRST CRIMES

Unable to earn honestly all he needed to gratify his passion for gambling, Raymond soon drifted into the companionship of some professional thieves he had met in the army. From that time his downfall was rapid; he never earned another honest dollar. Like myself and many other criminals who later achieved notoriety in broader fields, he first tried picking pockets. He had good teachers and he was an apt

HOW RAYMOND CUT THE FAMOUS "GAINSBOROUGH" OUT OF ITS
FRAME

pupil. His long, slender fingers seemed just made for the delicate task of slipping watches out of men's pockets and purses out of women's handbags. Soon he had plenty of money and a wide reputation for his cleverness in escaping arrest.

Aside from his love for faro and roulette, Raymond was always a prudent, thrifty man. In those early days he picked pockets so skillfully and disposed of his booty to the "fences" so shrewdly that it was not long before he had enough capital to finance other criminals. The first manifestation of the executive ability which was one day to make him a power in the underworld was his organization of a band of pickpockets. Raymond's word was law with the little group of young thieves he gathered around him. He furnished the brains to keep them out of trouble and the cash to get them out if by chance they got in. Every morning they met in a little Canal Street restaurant to take their orders from him—at night they came back to hand him a liberal share of the day's earnings.

But even the enormous profits of this syndicate of pickpockets were not enough to satisfy Raymond's restless ambition. He began to cast envious eyes at men like my husband (Ned Lyons), Big Jim Brady, Dan Noble, Tom Bigelow, and other bank sneaks and burglars whom he met in the places where criminals gathered. These men were big, strong, good-looking fellows. Their work looked easy—it was certainly exciting. They had long intervals of leisure and were always well supplied with money. "If these men can make a good living robbing banks," thought Raymond, "why can't I?" It was through Raymond's itching to get into bank work that I first met him. One day he came into a restaurant where my husband and I were sitting, and Mr. Lyons introduced him to me. I myself saw little in him to impress me, but when he had gone my husband said: "That fellow will be a great thief someday."

AMBITIOUS TO BE A BANK BURGLAR

It was hard for a young man to get a foothold with an organized party of bank robbers, for the more experienced men were reluctant to risk their chances of success by taking on a beginner.

"No doubt you're all right," they told him, "but you can see yourself that we can't afford to have anybody around that hasn't had experience in our line of business. It's too risky for us, and it wouldn't be fair to you."

"But how am I going to get experience if some of you chaps don't give me a chance?" Raymond replied; but still he got no encouragement from my husband and his companions.

"All right," he finally said one day. "I'll show you what I can do—I won't be asking to be taken in with you; you will be asking me."

So Raymond, in order to get experience, cheerfully made up his mind to make his first attempt in that line alone. He broke into an express company's office on Liberty Street and forced open a safe containing $30,000 in gold. The inner box, however, in which the money was kept, proved too much for Raymond's limited experience. To his great disgust, daylight came before he was able to get it open.

Tired and mad, Raymond trudged home in the gray of the morning, dusty, greasy, and with his tools under his arm. The newspapers printed the full details of the curious failure to reach the funds in the express company's safe, and Ned Lyons and his companions guessed very quickly whose work it was. Meeting Raymond a few days later, they accused him of having done the bungling job. He admitted that the joke was on him, and they all laughed loudly at his effort to get some experience.

"You're all right," said Big Jim Brady. "You've got the right idea—that's the only way to learn; keep at it and you will make a name for yourself someday."

His next undertaking was more successful. From the safe of an insurance company in Cambridge, Mass., his native town, he took $20,000 in cash. This established him as a bank burglar, and he soon became associated with a gang of expert cracksmen, including Ike Marsh, Bob Cochran, and Charley Bullard.

ROBBING THE BOYLSTON BANK

Raymond was very proud of having gotten a footing among the big bank burglars, whom he had long looked upon with respect and

ROBBING THE BOYLSTON BANK

envy. After several minor robberies Raymond became uneasy, and declared that he wanted to do a really big job.

That would be worthwhile—something that would astonish the police and would merit the respect of the big professional bank burglars.

Being a native of Massachusetts, he decided to give his attention to something in his own state. He made a tour of inspection of all the Boston banks, and decided that the famous Boylston Bank, the biggest in the city, would suit him.

And, in picking this great bank, Raymond had indeed selected an undertaking which was worthy of his skill and daring.

On Washington Street Raymond's quick eye at once discovered a vacant shop adjoining the Boylston Bank. He rented this shop, ostensibly for a patent medicine laboratory, filled the windows with bottles of bitters and built a partition across the back of the shop. The partition was to hide the piles of debris which would accumulate as the robbers burrowed into the bank next door; the bottles in the window to prevent passersby seeing too much of the interior.

When news of this clever ruse of Raymond's came out in the papers after the robbery, I made a note of it and used the same idea years later in robbing an Illinois bank at its president's request. That is an interesting chapter in my life which I will give you soon.

Careful measurements had shown where the tunneling through the thick walls of the bank could best be bored. Work was done only at night, and in a week's time only a thin coating of plaster separated them from the treasure. The robbers entered the vault on Saturday night, broke open three safes which they found there, and escaped with a million dollars in cash and securities. After this crime America was not safe for Raymond, so he and his comrades, including Charley Bullard, fled to Europe.

In Paris Bullard opened a gambling house, and there Raymond lived when the criminal ventures from which he was amassing his first fortune permitted.

And now there entered into Raymond's life a very remarkable romance, which almost caused him to reform.

In one of the big Parisian hotels at this time was an Irish barmaid named Kate Kelley. She was an unusually beautiful girl—a plump, dashing blonde of much the same type Lillian Russell was years ago. Bullard and Raymond both fell madly in love with her.

The race for her favor was a close one, despite the fact that Bullard was an accomplished musician, spoke several languages fluently, and was in other ways Raymond's superior. The scales, however, were surely turning in Raymond's favor when the rumor that he was a bank robber reached Kate's ears.

Raymond admitted this was the truth. But he never attempted to take advantage of his friend Bullard by telling Kate that he also was a thief. That was characteristic of the man. Criminal though he was, he never stooped to anything mean or underhanded, and would stand by his friends through thick and thin. Instead of trying to drag Bullard to disappointment with him, he pleaded with Kate to forgive his past and to help him make a fresh start.

"Marry me," he urged, "and I'll never commit another crime. We'll go to some distant land and I'll start all over again in some decent, honorable business."

But Kate would not be persuaded. She could not marry a self-confessed thief—no, never! A month later she married Bullard, little dreaming how glad the American police would be to lay their hands on him. Raymond was best man at the wedding, and to his credit it should be said that the bridal couple had no sincerer well-wisher than he.

RAYMOND'S GREAT DISAPPOINTMENT

Kate never realized how she had been deceived until several years later, when Bullard was given a prison sentence for running a crooked gambling house. She got an inkling of the facts then and her husband confessed the rest. By this time, however, she had two little children, and her anxiety for them impelled her to become reconciled to the situation and stick to her husband. After his release they left the children in a French school, returned to this country, and took a brownstone house at the corner of Cumberland Street and De Kalb Avenue in Brooklyn. Here they installed all the costly furniture, bric-a-brac, and paintings which had made Bullard's gambling house one of the show places of Paris.

Soon afterward Raymond also came to America, although there was a price on his head for his share in the Boylston Bank robbery. He lived with Kate and Bullard until the latter's jealousy caused a quarrel. Then he went to London and laid the foundations for the international clearing house of crime which for years had its headquarters in his luxurious apartment in Piccadilly.

With Raymond's cool, calculating brain no longer there to guide him, Bullard became reckless and fell into the hands of the police. He was sentenced to twenty years in prison. For her own and her children's support his wife had nothing except the rich contents of the Brooklyn home. She tried various ways of making a living, with poor success, and was at last forced to offer a quantity of her paintings for sale in an art store on Twenty-third Street.

In this store one day she met Antonio Terry. His father was an Irishman, his mother a native of Havana, and he had inherited millions of dollars in Cuban sugar plantations. Young Terry was infatuated with Kate's queenly beauty, and he laid siege to her heart so ardently that she divorced her convict husband and married him. Two children blessed this exceedingly happy marriage. Before Terry died he divided his fortune equally among his wife, his own children, and the children she had by her first husband. Kate Terry lived until 1895, and left an estate valued at $10,000,000. She passed her last years in a magnificent mansion on Fifth Avenue, surrounded by every luxury,

Kate Kelley's refusal to marry Raymond was one of the great disappointments of his unhappy life. He married another woman, but I am sure he never forgot the winsome Irish barmaid who had won his heart in Paris. "What's the news of Kate?" used to be his first question whenever I arrived in London, and his face would fall if something prevented my seeing her on my last visit to New York. Had this woman become Raymond's wife I am confident that the whole course of his life would have been changed, and that the world would have something to remember him for besides an unbroken record of crime.

PLANNING THE GAINSBOROUGH ROBBERY

As I have said, Raymond had not been long in London before he had forced his way into a commanding position in the criminal world. The cleverest thieves of every nation sought him out as soon as they set foot in England. They sought his advice, carried out his orders, and gladly shared with him the profits of their illegal enterprises. Crimes in every corner of the globe were planned in his luxurious home—and there, often, the final division of booty was made.

No crime seemed too difficult or too daring for Raymond to undertake. It was his almost unbroken record of success in getting large amounts of plunder and in escaping punishment for crimes that gave the underworld such confidence in him and made all the cleverest criminals his accomplices. Another reason for his leadership was his unwavering loyalty to his friends. Raymond never "squealed"—he never deserted a friend. When one of his associates ran foul of the law he would give as freely of his brains and money to secure his release as if his own liberty were at stake. It was his loyalty to a friend—a thief named Tom Warren—which led to his bold theft of the famous Gainsborough portrait for which J. Pierpont Morgan later paid $125,000. Here is how it came about:

Warren was in jail in London for his share in one of Raymond's forgeries. He was a great favorite of Raymond's and Harry vowed he would have him out before his case ever came to trial. This, however, was no easy matter, because England is not like this country, where almost anyone can furnish bond. The bondsman in England must be a freeholder and of good reputation.

While Raymond was searching his fertile brain for some way out of the difficulty, he and an English thief named Jack Philips happened to be walking through Bond Street and noticed the large number of fashionable carriages stopping at Agnew & Company's art gallery. To satisfy their curiosity they entered the gallery and found that everybody was crowding about a wonderful portrait of the Duchess of Devonshire, painted by the master hand of the great artist Gainsborough.

It was Gainsborough's masterpiece, and the Agnews were considering a number of bids that had been made for the painting. They had one offer of $100,000 from an American, but they were holding it on exhibition in the belief that a still better bid would be made.

Raymond stood long and thoughtfully on the edge of the crowd, studied the painting, took in the doors, walls, windows, chatted with an attendant, and slowly sauntered out, swinging his cane.

"I have the idea," exclaimed Raymond the instant they were in the street again. "We'll steal that picture and use it as a club to compel the Agnews to go bail for Tom Warren."

"You don't want that picture," said Philips. "It's a clumsy thing to do anything with."

"Of course I don't want the picture—but Agnew does," Raymond replied. "If I get it and send word that Tom Warren, who is in jail, knows where it's hidden—don't you suppose Agnew will hurry down to Old Bailey Prison, bail poor Tom out mighty quick, and pay him something besides if Warren digs up the picture for him?"

"He might," admitted Philips.

"Why, of course he will," persisted Raymond. "And it's the only way I can see to make sure of getting Tom Warren out before he is called for trial. When they try him they'll convict him; and then it's too late."

Philips was not enthusiastic over the scheme. In the first place he thought it too risky. Even if they did succeed in getting the picture he feared it would prove an elephant on their hands. Raymond, however, was a man who seldom receded from a decision, no matter how quickly it had been made. He argued away Philip's objections and with the assistance of Joe Elliott, a forger whom they took into their confidence, they proceeded with their plans for the robbery.

HOW THE GREAT MASTERPIECE WAS STOLEN

It was decided to make the attempt on the first dark, foggy night. Elliott was to be the "lookout" and keep a watchful eye for any of the army of policemen and private detectives who guarded the gallery's treasures. Philips was to serve as the "stepladder." On his broad, powerful shoulders, the light, agile Raymond would mount like a circus performer, climb through a window and cut the precious canvas out of the frame. It was a job fraught with the greatest danger, for the gallery was carefully protected with locks and bars and, besides, no one could tell when a policeman or detective might appear on the scene.

A thick fog settled down on the city the night of May 15, 1876. Under its cover the thieves decided to make their descent on the gallery early the next morning.

Just as the clocks were striking three, Raymond stole cautiously into the alley at the rear of the Agnew gallery. Then he was joined after a judicious interval by his two comrades.

Elliott remained near the mouth of the alley to watch for "bobbies." Raymond and Philips stealthily made their way over the back fence and to a rear window, whose sill was about eight feet from the ground.

Straining his ears for any ominous sound, Philips braced his big body to bear Raymond's weight. Then he made a stirrup of his hand and Raymond sprang like a cat to his shoulders.

Crouching in the darkness, Elliott watched and waited while Raymond applied his jimmy to the window. "Click" went the fastenings—but not too loud. The sash was cautiously raised and Harry Raymond dropped to the floor inside. Unluckily for the owners of the Gainsborough, the watchmen were asleep on an upper floor. Raymond, with the clever thief's characteristic caution, first groped his way to the front door to see if he could unfasten it and thus provide a second avenue of escape for use in an emergency. But the locks and bars were too much for him and he gave up the attempt.

By the dim rays of his dark lantern he could see the gallery's pride—the famous Gainsborough, hanging on what picture dealers know as "the line"—that is to say, about five feet from the floor.

The place was as quiet as the grave. A sudden sound gave Raymond a start—but it was only a cat that came mewing out of the darkness. Outside a cab rattled by and the heavy tread of a policeman's feet echoed through the street.

Raymond procured a table, which he placed before the portrait. By standing upon it he was barely able to reach the top. With a long, sharp knife he carefully slashed the precious canvas from its heavy gold frame.

At one of the bottom corners Raymond's knife made a series of peculiar zigzags. Later he cut from the portrait a little piece that matched these jagged lines. This was to send to the Agnews as evidence that he really had the picture.

After cutting the picture out, Raymond rolled it up carefully, tied it with a string, and buttoned it underneath his coat. Then he went out the same way he had entered, being careful to close the window behind him. With his companions he returned to his Piccadilly house and hid in a closet the picture which he hoped would prove his friend's ransom.

Next morning all London was in a fever of excitement over the loss of the Gainsborough. The Agnews offered $5,000 for its return and soon increased the reward to $15,000. A hundred of the best detectives in Scotland Yard scoured the city for clues.

The crime was shrouded in mystery. The doors of the gallery had not been tampered with. The fastenings of a rear window were broken, but the watchmen averred that no thief could have entered there as they had been sitting close by all night.

In all London the only persons who had no theories to advance as to the Gainsborough's fate were Raymond, Philips, and Elliott. They quietly waited for the excitement to subside, realizing that with the public mind in its present state it was altogether too hazardous to think of attempting to negotiate for the picture's return.

Meanwhile something happened to make the Gainsborough of no use to Raymond—his friend Warren was released from jail through the discovery of a technicality in his indictment. The famous portrait now became a veritable "white elephant." Raymond dared not return it—he feared to leave it in storage lest someone recognize it. So he carried the roll of canvas with him about the world until later, when, through "Pat" Sheedy's aid, he returned it to the Agnews and secured $25,000 for his pains.

PAT SHEEDY'S PART

And that is the history of what happened to Gainsborough's famous "Duchess of Devonshire" painting, which is now in J. Pierpont Morgan's private art gallery on Madison Avenue, New York. As I said earlier in this article, Raymond, who stole it, neither wanted the picture nor the money it represented. Raymond cut that painting from its frame as an act of loyalty to a fellow thief who was in trouble—to use it as a powerful lever to make sure of getting Tom Warren out of prison.

And right here, before going further with the episodes of Raymond's remarkable career, let me explain the mystery of how "Pat" Sheedy, the New York gambler, happened to be the person who sold the stolen Gainsborough back to the Agnews.

Long before that "Pat" Sheedy and Harry Raymond had done much business together. After Sheedy had accumulated a fortune by gambling, he built up a large and exceedingly profitable business in the sale of stolen paintings. Through his wide acquaintance he formed a convenient connecting link between the rich men who could afford to buy rare paintings and the clever criminals who knew how to steal them. Raymond took up the stealing of paintings when he became too old and too well known to the police to attempt more profitable kinds of robbery, and it was through Sheedy that he disposed of most of them.

A number of years before Raymond died he met me in London and asked if I could do some business for him. Being in need of ready money, I readily agreed. He took me to his apartments and handed me two paintings which showed at a glance that they had been cut from their frames.

"I got these from a cathedral in Antwerp," said Raymond. "I want you to take them to New York and sell them to Pat Sheedy for $75,000. If he won't give that, bring them back to me. I'll pay you well for your time and trouble."

Accordingly I sailed for New York. By wrapping the pictures in some old clothes at the bottom of my trunk, I got them by the customs inspectors without any trouble. I had then never met Sheedy and it occurred to me that if I had to leave the pictures with him he might try to take advantage of my ignorance of art by substituting copies for the originals. So, before setting out for Sheedy's office in Forty-second Street, I took an indelible pencil and marked my initials, very small, on the back of each canvas.

As I had expected, Sheedy asked me to leave the pictures until the next day as he was not sure he could afford to pay $75,000 for them. The next day he put me off with some other excuse, and so it went on for two weeks until I felt sure something was wrong. Then one morning he handed me two pictures, saying:

"Sorry, but I don't think these are worth more than $10,000. If you'll take that for them, I'll buy them."

RAYMOND AND HIS YACHT

Of course, I told him my instructions were not to accept a cent less than $75,000, and if he didn't want to pay that I would have to take them back to London. I was about to roll them up when I chanced to think of looking for my initials. They were not there—Sheedy was trying to palm off cheap copies on me in place of the originals. Quick as a flash, I pulled out the revolver I always carried in those days; shoved it right under Sheedy's nose, and said:

"Come, Mr. Sheedy—hand over the original paintings I left with you, or I'll blow your head off!"

He was considerably amazed at this warlike nerve on my part, but still had nerve enough left to argue that those were the pictures I had given him. But I was not to be tricked like that. Finally he went into an adjoining room—I after him with the gun in my hand—pulled open a drawer and took out the canvasses which had my initials on the back.

I carried them back to London, where Raymond sold them for $75,000, of which he gave me $10,000. I sold many stolen paintings to Sheedy after that, but he never tried to take advantage of me again.

Raymond often used to tell me that all his bad luck dated from the night he stole the famous Gainsborough. If the portrait really was a "hoodoo" its evil influence was a long time in taking effect. The two or three years after his robbery of the Agnew gallery saw the most daring crimes of his life and the money they yielded made him a multi-millionaire. Even his heavy losses at Monte Carlo could not seriously affect a fortune which was being steadily increased by all sorts of illegal undertakings.

He lived like a prince in London and Paris, owned several race horses and maintained, besides a sailing yacht, a palatial steam yacht with a crew of twenty men. He liked to vary the monotony of his cruises by deeds of piracy as sensational as any Captain Kidd ever attempted. On one such occasion he robbed a post-office on the island of Malta; on another he attempted to loot a warehouse on the docks at Kingston, Jamaica. This last exploit would have ended in his capture by a British gunboat which pursued him for twenty miles had his yacht not been a remarkably speedy craft.

RAYMOND'S EXPERT ON SAFE CRACKING

Raymond was a natural leader of men, and he had a sharp eye for able assistants. In his gangs were the greatest experts he could collect around him. Raymond was not a technically educated machinist, and he felt the need of an expert mechanic. For a number of years he watched the work of various other bank burglars and gave especial attention to any work that showed peculiar mechanical skill in getting into locks and steel safes.

Finally Raymond got his eye on a very promising young burglar named Mark Shinburn, who turned out to be a perfect wonder as a safe opener. Shinburn had served an apprenticeship in a machine shop and soon got a job in the factory of the Lilly Safe Company. Locks and safes had a peculiar fascination for Shinburn and he rapidly mastered the whole scheme, theory, and practice of lock-making, and knew the weak points not only of the locks his own company made but also of all the other big safe makers whose locks and safes were on the market.

Shinburn was just the man to fit into Raymond's band of experts. He had the peculiar and valuable technical knowledge that Raymond lacked. Raymond would select a bank, study the habits of the bank clerks, survey the situation, and lay out the plans for the job. Raymond would execute all these preliminaries and would lead his men into the bank and face to face with the safe; but at this point Shinburn would bring his genius into action and Raymond would stand by holding his dark lantern and watching Shinburn with silent admiration.

Raymond and Shinburn were the moving spirits of the bold gang which robbed the Ocean Bank in New York of a million dollars. With them were associated Jimmy Hope, who later led the attack on the Manhattan Bank; my husband, Ned Lyons; George Bliss; and several others.

On his return from a series of bank robberies on the Continent, Raymond took apartments in the house of a widow who lived with her two daughters in Bayswater, a suburb of London. He became in time much attached to this woman and her children, and lavished every luxury on them, including the education of the girls in the best French schools. For years this family never suspected their benefactor was a criminal, but supposed him to be a prosperous diamond importer.

When the eldest daughter's education was finished Raymond married her. She was a beautiful woman, but a weak, clinging sort of creature—very different from strong, self-willed Kate Kelley. Although passionately fond of her, Raymond's attitude toward her was always that of the devoted father rather than the loving husband.

After his marriage Raymond made many sincere attempts to reform. He became a student of art and literature, and for months at a time would live quietly in his London home or on board his yacht.

Then the old life would call him—he would mysteriously drop out of sight for a few weeks, and with the aid of some of his old associates add another crime to his record.

On one of these occasions he and John Curtin, a desperate burglar, went to Liege, Belgium. Their object was the robbery of a wagon which carried a large amount of valuable registered mail.

Raymond had fitted a key to the lock on the wagon and had sent a decoy package, whose delivery would necessitate the driver leaving the mail unguarded at a certain place. Curtin was to delay the driver's return while Raymond climbed up on the front of the wagon and rifled the pouches.

TREACHERY AND TRAGEDY

But Curtin carelessly failed to carry out part of this arrangement and the driver caught Raymond in the act. He was arrested, convicted, and given the first and only prison sentence he ever received—eight years at hard labor. With the loyalty for which he was famous Raymond steadfastly refused to reveal the identity of the confederate to whose folly he owed his own arrest, and Curtin escaped to England.

Soon after his sentence began, rumors reached Raymond in prison of the undue intimacy of his wife and Curtin. He investigated the reports and found them true. Raging with indignation at his wife's weakness and his friend's treachery, he broke his lifelong habit of loyalty, confessed to the authorities Curtin's share in the attempted robbery and told them where he could be found. Curtin was brought back to Belgium and sentenced to five years in prison.

Mrs. Raymond's mind gave way under its weight of remorse, and soon after her husband's release she died in an asylum. This was not the only crushing misfortune the released convict had to face. Through unfortunate investments and the dishonesty of friends he had trusted, his fortune had dwindled to almost nothing. He had to sell his yachts, his horses, and his London house with its fine library and art galleries in order to raise enough to provide for the education of his three children. He sent them to America, where they grew to manhood and womanhood in ignorance of the truth about their father.

"With an energy worthy of a better cause, Raymond at once set about making a new fortune. The whole world was his field—forgeries, bank robberies, and jewel thefts his favorite methods. But the nervous strain under which he had always lived and the long prison term were beginning to toll on him. His health was poor—his hand and brain were losing much of their cunning. Each crime made the next one more difficult, as the police got to know him and his methods better, and at last he was forced to abandon the bolder forms of robbery and devote his time entirely to the theft of famous paintings.

Yet, in the face of these handicaps, Raymond made in those last years of his life several fortunes. But one after another they were all swept away as quickly as they were made, and he died, as I have said, penniless.

Did crime pay Harry Raymond? He invested his natural endowment of brains, resourcefulness, daring, energy, and perseverance in criminal enterprises—and died a hunted, hungry, trembling outcast. One-half his industry and intelligence expended in honest business would have insured him a great and enduring fortune and a respected name. If crime does not pay for the really great criminals, how can the small criminals have any hope?

CHAPTER III

HOW I ESCAPED FROM SING SING, AND OTHER DARING ESCAPES FROM PRISON THAT PROFITED US NOTHING.

It is not easy to get out of Sing Sing Prison. Ned Lyons, the bank burglar, my husband, got out, and so did I. We were both serving sentences of five years at the same time.

Ned Lyons was a desperate man, and he had no notion of remaining long in any prison. Although his body was already considerably punctured with pistol bullets, he did not welcome the idea of inviting the rifle balls from the armed sentries who patrolled the prison walls on all sides. A dash for liberty was out of the question—if he was to escape it must be through some adroit scheme which would not make him a target for the riflemen who surround the prison.

My husband and I had a comfortable home on the East Side in New York, but I had very little peace of mind because of the activities of Lyons and his energetic companions. As I have said before, these men had found it very convenient to have my assistance in their various enterprises, and so it was that my husband and I both got into

Sing Sing at the same time—Lyons was confined in the men's prison and I was in the women's prison just across the road.

It was the Waterford, N. Y., bank that had been robbed of $150,000 and in the party were George Bliss, Ira Kingsland, and the famous Jimmy Hope. Of the whole party, Hope alone was not caught. Just how my husband got out of Sing Sing I am able to explain, because I myself planned the escape. The day I reached Sing Sing I was turned over to the prison physician for him to find out what my physical condition was, and what kind of work I was best fitted to do. This doctor's name was Collins. I shall never forget him for he was one of the kindest hearted men I ever knew. In my hope of being assigned to some easy work where I would be able to assist in my husband's plans for escape, I pretended to him I was suffering from all sorts of ailments.

PLANNING LYONS' ESCAPE

"Why, Doctor," I said, "I'm a sick woman, and besides I don't know how to do any kind of work. I've never had to work for a living."

"Well, my good little woman," the doctor replied, "you'll have to learn to work. You're in here for five years, and nobody is allowed to play the lady in Sing Sing Prison, you know."

"But, Doctor," I said, "you wouldn't have Sophie Lyons be anything but a lady, would you?"

"I'd like to make an honest woman of you, Sophie—that's more important than being a lady," he answered gravely, "and I'm going to try. I've got enough confidence in your sense of honor to give you a position as assistant nurse in the prison hospital. If you profit by your opportunities there, you can learn a good trade which will enable you to make an honest living when your term is up."

Nothing could have suited me better. A position in the hospital is the easiest work the prison offers, and it would give me just the opportunities I needed to help my husband escape. But I tried not to let Dr. Collins see how delighted I was and pretended to be very tearful and penitent as I thanked him for his kindness.

My husband was allowed to come and see me once a week under guard of a prison keeper. My conduct was so good and had given the matron and Dr. Collins such confidence in me that Ned and I were soon permitted to talk without any prison official being present to listen, as the prison rules required.

On these visits we had opportunity for discussing various plans for escape, but we both agreed that no one of them would probably succeed. I favored trying to get a forged pass—a counterfeit of the passes given to visitors, which the keeper at the prison door must have before he allows anybody to leave the building. But my husband had serious doubts.

About this time the matron's two children were taken sick and I was assigned to her house to take care of them. So faithfully did I nurse them back to health that the matron became quite fond of me and wanted me to remain there permanently as her personal servant.

When Ned Lyons came to see me again he was amazed at my good fortune in receiving a position which was the next best thing to liberty itself. It not only gave me all sorts of liberties but it enabled me to dress like any servant girl instead of in the regulation prison costume. This last fact would prove of tremendous advantage when my opportunity to make a break for liberty came.

Besides this I was allowed a little pocket money to buy candies, fruit, and occasional trinkets for the children.

Ned brought good news this time. He had pondered over my suggestion of a forged pass and the more he thought of it the more it seemed a promising scheme. But there were several important things that must be done, and done well, to make the plan reasonably sure of success.

Lyons, in prison, could not personally attend to the necessary details. He must have outside help. Usually, in such emergencies, I was the one who was relied upon to attend to matters of this kind—but, unfortunately, I, too, was in prison and under close watch.

So, in casting about for a reliable friend, Lyons decided to ask the help of "Red" Leary, the bank burglar, who had been associated with my husband in the famous $3,000,000 Manhattan Bank robbery. Word was sent to Leary and, on the next "visitors' day," a gentleman with high silk hat and black gloves and a lawyer's green bag drove up to the prison and sent in his card to the Warden—could Ned Lyons's "lawyer" see his imprisoned client?

In this guise "Red" Leary, high hat, lawyer's bag and gloves, swept into the prison and was courteously allowed an interview with my husband. Ned explained that two important things were needed—a visitor's pass properly signed with the "Warden's signature, and a carefully selected disguise for the escaping man to use. Could "Red" Leary attend to these two matters? "Red" Leary could, and with much pleasure—and the first move in the proceedings then and there was to carefully chew up his pass into a wad and tuck it behind his upper molar teeth.

Ned Lyons was led back to his cell and his "lawyer" put on his silk hat and arose to leave. He began searching his pockets and his green bag for his missing pass. An attendant helped him. Then the keeper at the door took a hand and looked through his pocketbook and papers while the "lawyer," in much distress, turned his pockets inside out. But no pass could be found.

At last the principal keeper, Connaughton, was called and he reprimanded the "lawyer" severely for his carelessness, but finally allowed the visitor to depart—and behind "Red" Leary's back teeth was the pass that was so much needed in forging a fresh one, with the proper day and date on it. Leary returned to New York and enlisted the services of a friend who was an expert check forger and soon had a pass that the Warden of Sing Sing himself would not know was a forgery. And this precious piece of paper was smuggled in to Lyons and he hid it in a crack in the floor of his cell. Ned planned to use this pass in making his escape if he could get a wig to cover his closely cropped head, a false beard to disguise his face, and a suit of clothes to replace his prison stripes in time for the next visitors' day.

"Red" Leary was to call to see me the next day and I was to arrange with him about securing these necessaries. They were to be left in an obscure corner grocery outside the prison where a "trusty," whom my husband had befriended, would claim them and smuggle them into Ned's cell.

It was a Wednesday I had my last call from Ned. Through one of those mysterious underground channels which keep the inmates of every prison in such close touch with the outside world, my husband had learned that on the following Tuesday, which was a visitors' day, the Warden and several other prominent officials of the prison were to be away attending a political meeting. That was the day he had set for his escape, provided our friend Leary could deliver the necessary disguise in time.

I had my doubts about "Red" Leary, who was good hearted enough and meant well, but was prone to be careless about keeping appointments. To my delight, however, he was on hand next day and he got permission from the matron to see me. When I asked him if he had everything in readiness he burst into a torrent of eager explanations.

"It's all out there in the buggy, Sophie," he said, "tied up in a bundle that you'd take for anything but what it is. Everything's there and everything's right. Why, even the shirt and collar are Ned's right size, and, say, I bet they'll feel good after rubbing his neck for months against that rough prison stuff."

THE PRISON BELL SOUNDS ALARM

Leary was a talkative fellow and he was going on with a detailed description of the wig and false beard which he had had made to order for the occasion, when Dr. Collins and the matron appeared at the end of the corridor where we were sitting. I signaled "Ned" to keep quiet and led him over to a window.

There, under pretext of showing him some geraniums I was trying to coax into bloom, I hurriedly explained where he was to leave the things and sent him away on the errand which meant so much to Ned and me.

The next Tuesday was the longest, most nerve racking day of my life. I had slept little the night before. All night long my mind was turning over Ned's plans—how, by feigning sickness, he would get permission to leave the shop and go to his cell; how he would change his clothes and put on the wig and false beard "Red" Leary had bought; and how, just as his fellow prisoners were being marched in to their noonday meal, he would mingle with the little crowd of departing visitors, surrender his forged pass at the gate and walk out of the main entrance of the prison a free man.

I had approved every bit of this plan—in fact, I myself had mapped out a large part of it. Yet now, when I considered on what narrow margins its success depended, I felt it was foredoomed to failure. Ned would be caught in the act—he would be put in solitary confinement—perhaps he would be shot dead by some vigilant guard.

I arose unusually early that Tuesday morning and worked unusually hard—to hide my nervousness.

Nothing out of the ordinary happened to relieve the awful tension. Early in the morning I heard from one of the other prisoners that the Warden and his assistants had gone away for the day. This, of course, coincided with Ned's plans, but it brought me little relief, for I feared that perhaps the officers left in charge might, in the absence of their superiors, be unusually careful in guarding their convict charges.

Noon came and went and still I heard nothing to relieve my anxiety. "No news is good news," I kept saying to myself, and in this case the old adage really spoke the truth. If there was no excitement about the prison it was good evidence that Ned's absence had not been noted. And if they did not discover his absence until they came to lock the prisoners up for the night all was well, for by that time I knew Ned would be safe in his old haunts on the East Side, in New York City.

But there still remained the discouraging possibility that at the last minute some of his plans had miscarried and he had been obliged to postpone the attempt.

Night came and I was setting the table for the evening meal when I heard the sounds of some unusual excitement over in the men's prison, across the road. There was much running to and fro, keepers were shouting to each other and presently the prison bell began to ring frantically. The sound of the bell made my heart jump—it was never rung, I knew, except in case of fire or when a prisoner escaped.

"What on earth is that bell ringing for?" said the matron. I was just saying that I didn't know and was trying to hide my excitement when in rushed Dr. Collins, all breathless and worried.

"Heard the news?" he shouted. And before the matron could say yes or no out he burst with the whole story.

"Ned Lyons, the bank robber, has escaped!" he said. "He's been gone since noon and they never knew it until just now, when they went to lock him in his cell and found nothing there but his suit of stripes. It's the boldest escape there's been in years."

"According to all accounts he walked right out of the main gate, stepped into a buggy that was waiting, and drove off like a gentleman. Of course he was disguised, and so cleverly they say that one of the head gatekeepers bowed to him at the gate, thinking he was a member of that new legislative commission from Albany."

A great weight rolled from my heart—Ned was free! I managed to control my feelings and it was lucky I did, for the next instant I saw the matron point a warning finger in my direction, and at that the doctor lowered his voice so that I could hear no more.

NED LYONS IN DISGUISE

The next morning, of course, the whole prison knew of the escape.

"If I get out I'll have you out in a few weeks," Ned had promised, and every day I was expecting some word from him.

As time went on, the confidence the matron and the doctor had in me seemed to increase rather than diminish. Soon I was allowed to accompany the matron's little daughters on long walks through the grounds outside the prison, and even as far as the village.

On one of these walks my attention was attracted by the peculiar actions of an old Indian peddler. He was a copper-colored, long-haired old chief, with Indian baskets and strings of beads on his arms. As soon as the girls and I stepped out of the prison gate this queer look-ing, bent old man singled us out from all the rest of the crowd and began following us about, urging us with muffled grunts to buy some of the bead goods he carried in a basket strapped around his neck.

I thought he was crazy and told him very emphatically that I didn't want any of his trash. But this did not discourage him in the least, and he dogged our footsteps wherever we went.

At last—more to be rid of the old fellow than because I wanted anything he had—I selected from his stock a pair of bead slippers. As I handed him the money I felt him press a little folded slip of paper into the hollow of my hand. Quick as a flash I closed my fingers over it, and in that instant I recognized—under the old Indian peddler's clever disguise—my husband, Ned Lyons.

He had come back to the very gates of the prison from which he had escaped to bring this message to me!

Kate Leary, wife of "Red" Leary, the bank burglar, was coming to see me soon—so the note said. I was to have my plans for escape all ready to discuss with her.

Now, the only way of getting out of my prison I had been able to discover was through a door which led from a little used passageway in the basement of the matron's house to a point just outside the prison walls.

This door—a massive, iron-barred affair—was seldom if ever opened. The big brass key which unlocked it hung with other keys from a ring suspended at the matron's belt.

Kate Leary could easily have a duplicate of that key made, but first I must secure a model of the original. This wasn't a difficult task—I had often done similar tricks to aid my husband in his bank robberies. I slipped into the matron's room while she was taking a nap and took a careful impression of the key on a piece of wax.

In due time Kate Leary brought the key which had been carefully made from my wax model. At the first opportunity I tried it—it fitted the rusty old lock perfectly! Hiding the key away as carefully as I ever hid any stolen diamonds, I waited impatiently for the night set for my escape.

It came at last. Between 6 and 7 o'clock was the hour, because then my household duties frequently took me into the vicinity of the basement door. It was a crisp December evening. It had snowed heavily all day, and it was still snowing and was growing colder.

About 6:30 I heard a peculiar low whistle. That was the signal that the pair of horses and the sleigh which were to carry me away were waiting outside.

There was, of course, no opportunity to get my hat and coat. Luckily I was all alone in the lower house—upstairs I could hear the matron and her family laughing and talking over their dinner.

Putting down the tray of dishes I was carrying I snatched the key from its hiding place under a flour barrel and hurried noiselessly along the dark passageway to the door that led to liberty.

My heart was thumping with excitement—my fingers were trembling so that I could hardly find the keyhole. It seemed ages before the lock turned and I stepped out into the cold winter night.

Although every second was precious, I took the time to close the door behind me and lock it. By thus concealing the way I had gone I would delay my pursuers just so much.

From an open window above me floated the voice of one of the matron's little daughters as I picked my way through the snow, bareheaded and with house slippers, avoiding the regular path.

"Mamma," she was saying; "why doesn't Sophie bring the rest of my dinner?"

"She'll bring it in a minute," the mother replied.

I heaved a sigh of relief—quite evidently my absence had not yet caused any suspicion.

Hurling the key into a snowdrift, I ran to the waiting sleigh. Ned was standing beside the sleigh with a big warm fur coat outstretched in his arms.

Without a word I slipped into the coat, hopped into the sleigh, and Ned gave the horses a clip with the whip and away we dashed toward Poughkeepsie.

The long fur coat and stylish hat which Ned had brought made me look like anything but an escaped convict. After a good warm supper at Poughkeepsie, we took the night train for New York and reached there safely the next morning.

And so we were free!

But what had we gained by our escape? We shall see.

When my husband first suggested his escape from Sing Sing he promised me that if he ever succeeded in getting out he would give up crime and turn to some honest and honorable work. That promise was made while his remorse was sharpened by his sudden change from high living to poor prison fare, and I was now to see how weak his good intentions really were.

After a few weeks in New York, where we received the warm congratulations of many friends on our escape from Sing Sing, we went to Canada to visit our children who were in school there. It was not long before our funds began to get low. I thought this a favorable time to remind my husband of his promises and to urge him to get some honest employment. But he would not listen to me.

"That would be all very well if I had any money," he said; "but I can't settle down until I have enough capital to give me a decent start. Wait until I do one more good bank job and then I will think about living differently."

AN "EASY" BANK ROBBERY

I agreed to this reluctantly, for I felt a premonition that when this "one more job" was finished we should both find ourselves back in Sing Sing again. And, as it turned out, I was right.

It was not altogether lack of money or the desire to live a decent life which made me plead with Ned to reform. The fact that there was a reward on both our heads and that at any minute some ambitious detective was liable to recognize us was beginning to tell on my nerves. Ned used to try to laugh my fears away by saying that I saw policemen in my sleep. Probably I did—at any rate, I know that for months, asleep or awake, I would jump at the slightest sound, thinking it was an officer come to take us back to Sing Sing. We could not live natural lives but had to be constantly dodging about, and occasionally running to cover for long intervals.

The "one more job" my husband had in mind was the robbery of a Montreal bank. He looked the ground over, found it to his liking, and then sent for a friend of ours, Dave Cummings, an experienced bank robber, to come on from New York and help us.

It was really a very simple undertaking for three such expert criminals as we were. My part of it was merely to stand in the shadow of an alley and watch for the possible return of one of the bank's two watchmen. There was small chance of his putting in an appearance, for my husband had previously cultivated his acquaintance, and on this particular evening had been plying him with mugs of ale until he had left him fast asleep in a nearby saloon.

Inside the bank there was a second watchman. He was an old man, but when he discovered Ned and Dave crawling through the rear window, which they had opened with their jimmies, he put up such a stiff fight that they had all they could do to stun him with a blow on the head, stuff a handkerchief down his throat, and tie his hands and feet with a piece of rope. As it was, they made so much noise that I nearly had nervous prostration in the alley where I was crouching half a block away.

"I think I'd better keep an eye on this old chap while you get the coin, Dave," my husband said, ruefully rubbing a bruised cheek he had received in the tussle with the faithful guardian of the bank.

So, as a matter of precaution, my husband mounted guard with his revolver over the watchman, while Dave solved the combination of the safe. Nothing further happened to interfere with our plans and by daybreak we were well on our way toward the Canadian border.

We had expected to get at least $30,000 from this robbery, but when we came to empty the satchel in which Dave had placed the plunder, we found there was not quite half that amount. It was all Dave's fault, as we learned later from the newspapers. He had carelessly overlooked a bundle of currency containing $25,000. I had always considered Dave Cummings a thoroughly careful and reliable man, but this expensive oversight of his rather shook my confidence in him.

My husband and I returned to New York with our share of the booty. There, a few days later, we were arrested, but not for the bank robbery in Montreal. The detectives who had been searching for us ever since our escape from Sing Sing had found our hiding place at last, and they took us back to prison to serve out our terms.

In our prison cells, once more, we had ample opportunity to consider how fruitless of results our escape had been. For all the risks we had run in getting out and for all the worrisome months we had spent in dodging detectives we had nothing to show except the fleeting satisfaction of a few days with our children. What had we gained! Nothing.

HOW BULLARD GOT OUT

A criminal's reputation for cleverness among his fellows depends very largely upon his ability to escape—or to help his friends to escape. Mark Shinburn used to take more pride in the way he broke into the jail at White Plains, New York, to free Charley Bullard and Ike Marsh, two friends of his, than he did in some of his boldest robberies.

After reconnoitering the ground and carefully planning the jail delivery, Shinburn and his companion, Raymond, put in a hard night's work burrowing into the jail. They took Marsh and Bullard out, but what was gained? Marsh was soon in trouble again and Bullard was taken again and ended his days in prison.

And now one more instance—a very curious one.

Of all the ways by which thieves have cheated the law out of its due, the most ingenious was probably the way "Sheeney Mike" brought about his release from the Massachusetts State Prison. He feigned illness so cleverly that the eminent physicians of the State Medical Board pronounced him suffering from a mysterious and incurable disease and ordered his release after he had served only three years of his twelve-year sentence for one of his daring burglaries.

It was the robbery of Scott & Co.'s silk warehouse in Boston that sent "Sheeney Mike" to Charlestown Prison, from which he so ingeniously escaped. He discovered that the watchman was vigilant all through the night except between the hours of 12 and 1 o'clock, when he went out to get something to eat. Mike secured a false key which unlocked a door to the warehouse, and arranged for two trucks to be on hand at a few minutes past 12 one night.

When the truckmen arrived they found Mike at the door of the warehouse coolly smoking a cigar. Quite naturally they thought he was the proprietor. After helping the men to load the trucks with $20,000 worth of expensive silks, "Sheeney Mike" turned out the lights, locked the door, and drove away to Medford, a suburb of Boston, where the goods were unloaded.

Before Mike found an opportunity to ship his plunder to New York he was arrested, found guilty, and sentenced to fifteen years in prison.

He tried every means of escape he could think of without avail. At last, in his desperation to get out, he began drinking large quantities of strong soap suds. This made him deathly sick and unable to retain any nourishment. His sufferings became so intense that he had to be removed from his cell to the prison hospital.

In the prison hospital the doctor in charge began watching his patient to be sure that some trick was not being played on him. A careful examination of Mike revealed no organic trouble—the doctor could find no reason for the strange symptoms. And yet right in front of his eyes Mike would be taken with violent pains in the stomach, followed by vomiting.

The prison doctor was worried. He gave stomach tonics. Still the spasms and nausea continued. He put his patient on a cereal diet—but his vomiting was not lessened. He changed the diet; he gave beef juice; he changed it to milk and brandy—nothing brought relief.

The prison doctor was worried. Here was this once vigorous man wasting away to a pallid skeleton in spite of his best efforts. The doctor was a conscientious man and he called a consultation of two outside physicians at his own expense. They patiently went over the record of the case and examined "Sheeney Mike" minutely—there was nothing to account for the patient's alarming condition. Still, it might possibly be this or that, and so they would recommend trying a few things that had not yet been tried by the prison doctor.

"SHEENEY MIKE'S" ESCAPE

"Sheeney Mike" thought that the time had come for some new manifestation of his mysterious disease which would still further puzzle and frighten the doctor, so, as the new treatment of the consulting doctors was begun, Mike made preparation for some new symptoms. He scraped an opening in his right side and each night rubbed salt and pepper into it. He soon had an angry looking inflammation which shortly produced a flow of pus. When Mike had reached this achievement with his sore he languidly called the doctor's attention to it.

This new development was enough. The doctor sadly shook his head. Things were going from bad to worse.

"My poor man," he said, "you probably haven't a month to live—certainly not in this prison. You might improve if you had your freedom; I don't know. I am convinced that it would be murder to keep you here. I shall at once recommend to Governor Butler that you be pardoned. I decline to have your death on my conscience any longer."

On the ground that the patient could not possibly live more than a few weeks in prison all three doctors solemnly certified to the Governor that "Sheeney Mike" was a dying man and recommended immediate pardon. Governor Butler approved the recommendation, and next day out walked "Sheeney Mike" free, pardoned and restored to full citizenship. Soap suds, a little salt, and a sprinkling of pepper had opened the bars for him.

But what did "Sheeney Mike" gain by all this? Nothing.

He had his freedom and a laugh on the doctors—but his astonishing persistence in his soap-sud poisoning had so undermined his health that he never recovered his strength and he finally died in Bellevue Hospital in great agony after a long and painful illness.

And now one more case—also unusual and remarkable.

Of course, the escape of Eddie Guerin, a few years ago from Devil's Island surprised everybody and attracted a great deal of attention. Guerin is a well-known thief who has operated in England, America, and more or less all over Europe. Guerin, with a companion, robbed a bank in Lyons, France, of $50,000, and a little later stole $30,000 from the American Express Company in Paris. These two jobs were too much for the French police, and they grabbed Guerin.

Guerin, traveling under the name of Walter Miller, and assisted by an accomplice, entered the American Express Company's office in Paris under the pretense of transacting some business. The other man busied himself attracting the attention of the agent while Guerin sprang across the counter with a drawn pistol. At this moment the agent and a couple of clerks noticed Guerin's peculiar activity, but they were unable to make any outcry or move because Guerin's accomplice kept the express company's employees covered with a couple of revolvers. Guerin helped himself to $30,000 which was lying within reach in an open safe, and then the two thieves coolly walked out the door.

Guerin was caught and convicted of the express company robbery, and sentenced to fourteen years imprisonment in the French penal colony on Devil's Island, off the coast of South America. This is the place where Captain Dreyfus, the French army officer, was imprisoned, and it has been the boast of the French police that nobody can escape from Devil's Island.

Guerin had served four years of his sentence before he succeeded in maturing a plan for escape. He had the friendship of a notorious woman known as "Chicago May," who collected a fund in New York's underworld and managed to get the money into Guerin's hands on Devil's Island. By the judicious use of this money Guerin arranged for the escape of himself and two other prisoners, French convicts, whom he decided would be helpful to him in the journey through the swamps and wildernesses after they left the penal colony.

The prison officials who had been reached by Guerin's fund arranged to have him and his fellow convicts sent under guard to the outermost part of the Island, which is a dense swamp, full of malaria and poisonous snakes and insects. The next day the guards, who had been well paid, buried a dead convict in the prison cemetery, and over the grave they set up a headboard bearing the name "Eddie Guerin." This was to complete the records of the prison, and a duly certified copy of the prison record, telling of Guerin's death and burial, was forwarded to France.

This much accomplished, Guerin and his two companions were allowed to get away from the guards and they were soon lost in the swamp. They were allowed to carry some tools, water, and provisions. While the guards made a feeble and perfunctory search in the swamps the three convicts set to work busily completing a boat and paddles. When these were finished they loaded the boat with their food supplies, launched it and headed along the South American coast for Dutch Guiana, the three men paddling and sleeping by turns.

I have heard Guerin's own account of his escape, and I will repeat it just as he told it.

Guerin was armed with a revolver and cartridges, fortunately, as otherwise all his planning would have been in vain. After a day or two in the boat he noticed that his two companions were growing very chummy. They were astonishingly willing to do the paddling and let him sleep.

So one night Guerin feigned to be asleep but kept an eye and both ears open. Presently he heard his companions talking together in Spanish, which they had no reason to believe he understood.

The men whom he had helped out of prison had made up their minds that he had a lot of money left. They were conspiring to slit his throat as he slept, rob his body, and feed him to the sharks. The men lost no time in putting the enterprise into operation. But, as they crept upon him, knives in hand, they found themselves looking into the muzzle of his revolver.

"For three days and nights," Guerin has told, "I could hardly lower the muzzle of my revolver, and for them to stop paddling would mean only prolongation of the agony of our escape."

At last all were so exhausted that they decided to try to rig a sail by tying their shirts to an oar. A breeze had sprung up and a moderately large sea was now endangering the craft. Everywhere about the boat were big man-eating sharks. These creatures swam around the boat, frequently whirling over on their backs and snapping their jaws within reaching distance of the little craft.

One of Guerin's companions began to complain about his eyes, and the reflection of the fierce tropical sun on the water had almost blinded all three convicts. Suddenly this man stood up in the boat and pressed his sun-burned hands to his eyes. He groped for a moment about him like a blind man, and then lost his balance and fell to the side of the canoe. The boat heeled over and began to take water over the side and Guerin and this companion were thrown into the water. A shark close by made a dash for Guerin's companion, and this gave Guerin a chance to clamber back into the canoe, as another shark swept around the stern, narrowly missing the American burglar.

HORRORS WORSE THAN DEATH

The tragic end of one of the party terrified Guerin and the remaining convict, and put an end to the conspiracy against Guerin. But the straining of the canoe when it had nearly upset and the rising sea had made the boat begin to leak. Guerin and his fellow voyager decided that they could not risk it any longer in the boat, but must make a landing and continue their journey through the swamps and wildernesses and run the risk of encountering hostile natives.

After the canoe was beached they hauled it up on shore and hid it among the trees so as to leave no track in case a searching party should follow after them. They had no very definite idea of the proper direction to follow—knowing only that they were on the wild coast of Dutch Guiana, and must travel inland several miles to find a settlement. Both men were as thin as skeletons, worn out with bailing and paddling the leaky boat, and their scanty food supply was scarcely fit to eat. They plunged haphazard into the tropical forest and swamp. They had nothing to mark the time but the sun, which was sometimes completely hidden by the dense foliage. Threading cautiously through the swamps and forests filled with treacherous death traps, they were terrified and tortured by the constant presence of poisonous snakes and venomous insects and lizards. Describing this trip, which lasted several days, Guerin said:

"After a while we seemed to be struggling through an endless maze, that was leading in the end to nowhere, and this sort of thing went on and on. Sometimes the undergrowth, waist high, would rustle as an invisible snake took flight before us. The next moment we would be floundering in a quagmire, not knowing whether to go back or to the left or to the right, and conscious of sinking deeper with each second of indecision."

"With throbbing head, burning skin, chattering teeth, aching and leaden limbs, we were inclined to throw ourselves down to miserably die, and we knew that the swamp fever was upon us."

Finally, Guerin and his companion reached a river and concluded that they would follow its bank in the hope of coming upon a native camp, where they would take chances of a friendly or unfriendly reception. Before long their bloodshot eyes beheld a hut. As they approached it, swaying and trembling from their hunger and hardships and fever, a black native emerged and set up a shout which soon collected many other blacks from neighboring huts, who rushed at them with spears.

Guerin could not understand their language, but endeavored to explain to them that they wanted food, rest, and a guide. Guerin's companion, in an effort to make plain their willingness to pay for what they wanted, showed a couple of francs in silver. This was an unfortunate move, because it excited the cupidity of the blacks, who promptly fell upon them and searched them and took away everything they had of value, after which they were pushed into a hut and kept prisoners.

Sick, weak, almost discouraged, Guerin and his companion managed to escape, and, stumbling through the treacherous morasses, emerged in the neighborhood of an Indian village. Unlike the blacks, these natives greeted the strangers in a friendly manner and invited Guerin and his companion to stay with them until they were rested and able to continue their journey. After a few days Guerin and the other convict were given a guide by the Indians and he piloted them to a seaport, where they embarked on a boat loading for New Orleans. From New Orleans Guerin went to Boston, and then took passage for England, hoping to find the woman he had been in love with when he was sent away to Devil's Island. Guerin found her, but she was then the sweetheart of another.

In the row that followed this woman and her lover tried to shoot Guerin.

And so Eddie Guerin escaped—but he purchased his freedom at a frightful cost of agony and ruined health.

Does crime pay? Nobody will claim that it does if the criminal gets into prison. But criminals often escape from prison, it is urged—what then? And it is to answer this question that I have endeavored to take the public behind the scenes and show them the real truth about a few famous escapes from prison, and how the escaped convicts profited nothing, but were, indeed, worse off than they were before.

CHAPTER IV

WOMEN CRIMINALS OF EXTRAORDINARY ABILITY WITH WHOM I WAS IN PARTNERSHIP

Sophie Lyons, bank president—can you imagine it? Strange as it may seem, I actually held such a position in New York City for several months, and the experience proved one of the most surprising in my whole career.

Although this venture in high finance yielded me only a bare living and nearly landed me in a prison cell, it gave me a remarkable insight into the methods used by clever women to swindle the public, and showed me how these women are able to carry through schemes which the most skillful men in the underworld would never dare undertake.

All this happened in the days before I had won the wide reputation which my crimes later gave me. I had come to New York with very little money and with no definite plans for getting any—my husband was serving a term in prison and I was temporarily alone and on my own resources.

Walking up Broadway one day, I came face to face with Carrie Morse, a woman I knew by reputation as one of the most successful swindlers in the business. Friends of mine had often pointed her out to me, but we had never been introduced, and I had no idea that she knew me.

I was, therefore, greatly surprised when she stepped up to me and called me by name; "Why, Sophie Lyons, how do you do!" she said, with the well-bred cordiality which was such an important part of her stock in trade. "Come in and have some tea with me."

As we entered a well known restaurant I noted with envious eyes the evidences of prosperity which Carrie flaunted. From the long ostrich plume which drooped from her Parisian hat to the shiny tips of her high-heeled shoes, she was dressed in the height of fashion and expense. At her throat sparkled a valuable diamond brooch, and, when she removed her gloves, there flashed into view a princely array of rings which made my own few jewels look quite cheap and insignificant.

WE PLAN TO START A BANK

And yet, except for this somewhat too lavish display of jewelry, there was nothing loud or over-dressed about her. It was plain that she knew how to buy clothes, and her tall, well-rounded figure set off her stylish garments admirably. In every detail—her well kept hands, her gentle voice, her superb complexion, and the dainty way she had of wearing her mass of chestnut hair—she was the personification of luxury and refinement. As she looked that day Carrie Morse would have passed anywhere without the slightest question for the beautiful and cultured wife of some millionaire.

All these facts, which I took in at a glance, made me less inclined to question too closely the motives which had prompted her to hail me as an old friend when we had never had even a speaking acquaintance. Quite evidently she had lots of money or an unlimited line of credit. How did she get it? That was what I was curious to find out. I made up my mind that I would be just as nice to her as I knew how—hoping that I might learn from her a new and easy road to wealth.

By the time our tea was served we were chatting away like old friends.

"Sophie," she said, "I'm going to take you into my confidence and help you make a lot of money. You and I will start a bank."

"You mean, rob a bank, don't you!" I said, not quite able to believe my ears.

"I mean nothing of the sort," she said, setting down her teacup with a thump. "You and I will start a bank. It will be a bank for ladies only. Any woman who has a little money saved up can come to us for advice. We will take her money and show her where she can invest it so that she will get more interest than she could in any other way."

"But I don't know anything about running a bank," I protested. "I'm Ned Lyons' wife— he and I are bank robbers, not bank owners."

"That's all right," she reassured me. "It's not necessary for you to know anything about running banks in order to hold the position I have in mind. All you have to do is to follow my instructions—and you'll soon be wearing as many diamonds as I am."

A half hour before I should have thought it the height of absurdity for anyone to suggest my engaging in a wild-cat banking scheme with Carrie Morse. Yet now I sat spellbound by her magnetic power—patiently listening to details which were all Greek to me and getting from every word she uttered renewed confidence in the reality of the financial castles in the air which were to make us both millionaires.

What a business woman Carrie Morse would have made! With her personal charms, her eloquence, and her quick ingenuity she had no need to depend on crime for a living—she could have accumulated a fortune in any legitimate line of work.

I ENTER "HIGH FINANCE"

The upshot of it all was that I agreed heart and soul to Carrie Morse's plans for taking a short cut to fortune. First, she had excited my avarice by her stories of the ease with which money could be made; then she dazed me by her apparent familiarity with the intricacies of finance. At last I became as credulous as any farmer is when he comes to the city to exchange a few hard earned dollars for ten times their value in green goods.

I accompanied Carrie to the door of her hotel. The fact that she was staying at the fashionable Brunswick, while I was finding it hard work to raise the price of a room at a modest hotel farther downtown, proved another argument in favor of my following the leadership of my new found friend.

"Meet me at 9 o'clock tomorrow," Carrie had said, "at No.____ West Twenty-third Street."

I was on hand a few minutes before the appointed hour. The address she had given me was a three-story brownstone-front house just beyond the business section of the street. But I was barely able to see it through the clouds of mortar dust raised by a gang of workmen who were busily engaged in tearing out the whole front of the building.

"Yes, this is No.____," said one of the workmen to whom I addressed a rather startled inquiry. "We're making it over into offices." I was convinced that I had made a mistake in the address and was just on the point of turning away when I saw Carrie Morse coming down the steps.

"Good morning," she called cheerily. "This is the new bank—or, rather, it will be when these workmen get it finished. And you, my dear, are no longer Sophie Lyons, but Mrs. Celia Rigsby, the president of this rich and prosperous institution for the amelioration of the finances of the women of New York."

"But," I said, beginning now for the first time to feel some doubts about the undertaking in which I had so suddenly embarked, "where is all the money coming from to start this bank?"

"Money?" said Carrie, lowering her voice to a hoarse whisper, "Don't speak of that so loud—the workmen might hear you. I've leased this house and I'm having all these alterations made on credit. I haven't a cent to my name—that's why I'm starting this bank. I need money and this is the easiest way I know to make it."

Carrie's easy confidence allayed most of my fears and I forgot the rest when, from some mysterious source, she produced money enough to support me in comparative luxury during the ten days we had to wait for the bank to be completed. She insisted that there was absolutely nothing for me to do in the meantime and that she didn't want to see me on Twenty-third Street until the bank was ready for business.

I was hardly prepared for the surprises which I found when I visited the bank on the appointed day. Over the entrance hung a huge brass sign reading,

"New York Women's Banking and Investment Company." The entire front of the building had been remodeled into a commodious and up-to-date counting room. This was lighted by two large plate glass windows and the entrance was through a massive door whose glass was protected by heavy bars. These bars looked for all the world like iron, but Carrie assured me that they were only wood covered with tin and painted black.

Inside were all the appurtenances of a first-class banking establishment—brass railings, desks, counters, chairs, and, in the most conspicuous position, an enormous "burglar proof" safe. In the rear were partitioned off two little private offices, their doors labeled "Mrs. Celia Rigsby, President," and "Mrs. Carrie Morse, General Manager."

All this quite took my breath away, but what impressed me most of all was the sight of half a dozen old graybeards who were busily engaged on some bulky account books. Not one of these men could have been less than sixty years old and all were of venerable aspect, with spectacles, white hair, and long, white beards.

"Why do you hire such old men?" I asked Carrie at the first opportunity. "And where do you get the money to pay all of them?"

"S-s-sh!" she whispered. "Don't you know there's nothing that inspires people's confidence like old men? Many people who would never trust their money to a young, active man will gladly hand it over to an old, venerable appearing fellow. And the next best thing to an old man is a pretty woman—that's why I think you and I shall make such a success of this business. As for paying these old men, they don't get a cent. They are all working for nothing in the hope of getting a chance to invest some money in the business."

HOW WE FOOLED THE PUBLIC

I was so impressed by these fresh evidences of Carrie's business ability and my own ignorance that I felt quite relieved when she informed me that I would not have to remain at the bank, but would fulfill my duties as president at some apartments she had taken for me in a fashionable quarter of Fifth Avenue. These apartments were furnished in splendid style and Carrie handed me a roll of bills with which to purchase some gowns that would be in keeping with my new home.

After my wardrobe was purchased and my trunks moved over from the hotel, I was not long in learning just what Carrie expected of me. She began inserting advertisements in all the leading newspapers offering "widows and other women of means" investments which were guaranteed to net them from 15 to 20 percent on their money."

When women called in answer to the advertisement at the bank on Twenty-third Street many of them would want more evidence than Carrie could supply before they would part with their money. These doubting ones were referred to me—Mrs. Celia Rigsby, if you please, who had made a fortune by investing her late husband's $1,500 insurance money in the securities offered by the Women's Banking and Investment Company.

The advertisements were kept going in the newspapers, and more and more women kept coming to the bank on Twenty-third street. Mrs. Morse received them all, talked many of them into leaving their money with her right then and there, and to those who had misgivings she said sweetly:

"But I would rather you would not be influenced by anything I have said. It is your duty to yourself to investigate and assure yourself as to just what profits we are really paying on investments. Perhaps you would like to see and talk with one of our customers who has done so well with our investments that she has taken an interest in our bank. I'm sure you'd be interested in talking with Mrs. Rigsby."

The style in which I lived on Fifth avenue left no doubt of my wealth, and, with Carrie's help, I soon had a glib and convincing story to tell of my previous poverty and the steps I had taken to reach my present prosperity.

Of course, I explained, I took no active part in the bank's affairs. I allowed the use of my name as president and permitted Mrs. Morse to refer prospective investors to me merely because I was so well satisfied with the way my own investments had turned out and felt a philanthropic desire to share my good fortune with other women.

Business increased rapidly and greater crowds of women came in reply to my partner's glowing advertisements. Many of them would hand over their money right away in exchange for a handful of the crinkly stock certificates which filled a whole room in the rear of the bank. These certificates were printed in all the colors of the rainbow, for, as Carrie naively explained, "some of the ladies prefer green, some blue, some black, and so on."

Carrie was jubilant. She kept me liberally supplied with money for clothes and the heavy expenses of my apartment, but when I asked her about a further share of the profits she said:

"Sophie, you're as ignorant as a new born babe of business methods. It's always customary to leave all the money in a new business until the end of six months. Then we'll divide what we've made, turn the bank over to someone else and go to Europe for a long rest."

I had my doubts about the truth of this, but, as I was making a good living with little effort and had nothing better in sight just then, I determined to continue under Carrie's leadership. She continually reassured me by insisting that what we were doing was just as legitimate as any business and that there was nothing in it for which the police could take us to task.

Although I foolishly had confidence in Carrie's ability to keep out of trouble, I did not for a minute believe that the securities she was selling were worth the paper they were printed on. Still, as most of the women who called to see me seemed to be persons of means who could well afford to contribute toward our support, I did not feel any serious compunctions at advising them to invest. It seemed no worse than picking a rich man's pocket or robbing a wealthy bank—and it was not half so difficult or so hazardous to life and liberty.

OUR BANKING BUBBLE BURSTS

One day, however, something happened that filled me with honest indignation at Carrie Morse and her schemes. A poor, bent old widow called to see me—a woman whose threadbare clothes and rough hands plainly showed how she had to struggle to make a living. Tied up in her handkerchief she had $500 which she had just drawn from a savings bank.

"It's all I have in the world," she said with tears in her eyes, "and I've had to scrimp and slave for every cent of it. I saw Mrs. Morse's advertisements and I've been to see her this morning. She says if I'll give my money to her she can double it for me in two years. Would I better do it? I'm only a poor old woman and I want you to give me your advice."

As diplomatically as I could I explained to her that, while Mrs. Morse's scheme was an excellent one, it would be much wiser for a woman in her circumstances to keep her money in the savings bank, and I made her promise that she would put it back there at once. Then I put on my hat and coat and hurried over to the bank to see Carrie Morse.

As usual Carrie was in the midst of an enthusiastic description of her stocks while a long line of women anxiously awaited their turn with her. I took her by the arm, led her into one of the private offices, and shut the door.

"Carrie Morse, this sort of business has got to stop," I said with all the emphasis I could. "I'm willing to help you swindle women who can afford to lose the money, but I positively will not have any part in taking the bread out of the mouths of poor widows like the one you just sent over to see me. Sooner than do that I'll starve—or go back to robbing banks or picking pockets."

"There, there—don't get excited," she said soothingly. "Perhaps I did make a mistake in encouraging the poor widow. But this is a business where you can't help being deceived sometimes. Often the women who plead poverty the hardest and dress the poorest really have the most money hidden away. I'll give you my word of honor, though, that I won't accept any money from that widow even if she tries to force it on me."

Somewhat mollified at this I started back home to renew my interview's with the prospective investors who came daily in crowds.

For several weeks things went on as before. Then one day I chanced to meet the poor widow who had so excited my sympathies. To my surprise she confessed that she had finally yielded to the lures of Mrs. Morse's advertisements and had given her $500 for some shares in a bogus western oil company.

I was indignant that Carrie should have forgotten her promise in that way, and I set out at once to demand an explanation. As I was approaching the bank my attention was attracted by some unusual excitement just outside the entrance.

Scenting trouble and thinking perhaps it would be just as well if I were not recognized in that vicinity I slipped into a doorway across the street where I could see what was going on without being seen.

Around the doors of the bank surged a crowd of several hundred very excited persons, mostly women. Among them I recognized many of the ladies whom I had urged to invest in Carrie's securities. I also noticed our landlord, the contractor who had altered the building, the man who had supplied the furniture, a collector for the gas company, and numerous other creditors of the bank.

The doors of the bank were closed and the closely drawn shades revealed no sign of life inside. In front of the doors stood three blue-coated policemen vainly trying to keep the pushing crowd back.

What interested me most was two Central Office detectives who mingled with the crowd trying to get some information from the hysterical women.

They made slow progress, for the women were too excited to do more than repeat over and over again the sad refrain: "My money's gone!" But the sight of those plain clothes men showed me the wisdom of getting out of the way before they had time to get too deep into the cause of all the trouble.

Quite plainly the bubble had burst. Some investor had become suspicious and the investigation which she or her husband had started had demolished the flimsy structure which Carrie's vivid imagination had reared.

Bitterly I thought of Carrie's treachery to me. Without a word of warning she had fled, leaving me alone and almost penniless to face arrest. By now she was doubtless on her way to Europe or Canada with all the money in which I should rightfully have shared.

There was only one thing for me to do—get away from my Fifth avenue house before any of the women investors recovered enough of their senses to put the police on my trail. Hurriedly throwing a few of my possessions into a trunk I shipped it to my friend Mr. Rowe's hotel and followed there myself on foot.

To Mr. Rowe I poured out the whole story of my troubles and asked his help. He was very willing to do all in his power to aid me.

"It looks bad for you, Sophie," he said. "A detective was here less than fifteen minutes ago inquiring for you and the chances are that he'll be back again before long. But I can easily hide you until night, and then we'll try to find some way of smuggling you to the station. I'll loan you whatever money you need and will ship your trunk to you when you get to Detroit."

Mr. Rowe was right—the detective returned and posted himself at the front door of the hotel. With him came another headquarters man to guard the side entrance. They were evidently convinced that Sophie Lyons was in the hotel or that she would soon return there.

HOW I ESCAPED ARREST

Night came and the two sleuths showed no signs of leaving. The only avenue of escape from the upper room where I had been hiding all day was by the window.

With Mr. Rowe's kind help I securely fastened to the window frame one end of a long rope, which was kept for use in case of fire. Down this I slid in the darkness to the roof of a one-story building adjoining the hotel. From there it was an easy drop to a little alley, which finally brought me out on Broadway.

After an agonizing wait of several minutes at the station I got safely on board a train and was soon speeding toward Detroit. Then I drew the first long breath I had taken since morning, when I had seen that tearful crowd of investors and creditors in front of the closed bank.

Carrie Morse was never caught or punished for the ladies' bank swindle, which the newspapers later said must have netted her at least $50,000. Years after I met her in Chicago where she was operating a matrimonial agency which was almost as crooked as the bank had been. She never mentioned our banking venture nor offered me my share of the profits, and, as I was prosperous then, I never asked her for it.

She was a swindler to her dying day and served many long prison terms. As she grew old it took all the money she could make to keep out of jail and she finally died in poverty. With all her cleverness she never seemed able to see what expensive folly it was to waste her really brilliant abilities in a life of crime.

This was my first experience with clever women swindlers. I was surprised to learn, to my sorrow, that the standards of good faith which are maintained among men of the underworld do not hold good among most women criminals. I fully determined to have no more dealings with criminals of my own sex.

But this wise resolve was broken quite by accident a few years later, while I was traveling in the south of Europe and became acquainted with Mrs. Helen Gardner, an English swindler and confidence operator. Mrs. Gardner was a woman of fine presence, a finely modulated voice, all the manners, graces, and charms of a well-bred English woman, and an amazingly inspiring and persuasive conversationalist.

In daring and ingenuity this remarkable woman surpassed any man I ever knew. Crimes which the cleverest men in the underworld would have declared impossible or too foolhardy to undertake she not only attempted, but carried through to success.

For years the boldest schemes followed one another in rapid succession from Mrs. Gardner's fertile brain. Swindling was as natural to her as breathing is to normal persons. She was the most successful confidence woman who ever operated in England or on the Continent, and no rich man was safe once she got her traps set for him.

I first met Mrs. Gardner in Nice, where I was enjoying a little vacation after a long, arduous bank robbing campaign in America. She was then traveling under the name of Lady Temple.

To make a long story short, we soon became great friends. We went everywhere together and she generously shared with me the luxuries with which she was so plentifully supplied. She finally even induced me to take rooms in the hotel adjoining her own suite.

I did not know at that time that she was Mrs. Gardner, the famous English confidence swindler.

She told me little of her personal affairs except that her husband, Sir Edward Temple, had been a prominent physician in London and that she was in Nice to recover from the shock incident to his sudden death. The deep mourning she habitually wore and the heavy black band on her visiting cards bore out this story, but, to tell the truth, I didn't bother my head much about its truth or falsity.

I did not at that time happen to know that it is the custom in England for a doctor's practice to be sold when he retires from business or dies.

There was no doubt that she had money and that she was giving me a liberal share of its benefits—why should I worry about where it came from or how long it would last?

I, in turn, kept her in equal ignorance of my own past life and of my means of support.

But there was one thing about which I couldn't help being very curious—the number of doctors who were calling at the hotel to see Lady Temple. Every day there was at least one and some days there were three or four—each came alone and the same one seldom appeared a second time.

MRS. GARDNER'S CLEVER SCHEME

Lady Temple invariably saw all of them. When a physician's card came up she would ask me to retire to my own rooms and then would be closeted for a long time with the visitor. It could not be professional calls these doctors were making, for there was nothing about her ladyship's health to call for such a varied assortment of medical attention.

What could be the meaning of all these visits from physicians? My curiosity got the better of me and I determined to do a little eavesdropping.

My opportunity came when the maid brought in the card of "Dr. Robert Mackenzie, of Edinburgh, Scotland." As usual, Lady Temple said, "Show him up," and asked me if I would be good enough to retire. Instead of closing the door which led from Lady Temple's sitting room to my own I left it open a trifle and stood there with my ear to the crack, where I could hear every word that was said and also get an occasional peep at the lady and her visitor.

Dr. Mackenzie was a grave, pompous appearing man, slightly under middle age. He was dressed in the conventional garb of the old school physician and carried a small medicine case.

"I have come to see you, Lady Temple," he said, after the usual polite preliminaries, "in relation to your advertisement in the current number of the Lancet. Your late husband's practice seems to offer just the opportunity I have long been seeking to establish myself in London. May I ask if it is still for sale?"

"My husband was a very distinguished man and had a very lucrative practice," the bogus Lady Temple replied. "You must read these notices in the papers which were printed when he died. Here is one from the London Times—oh! my poor dear husband!"

At this point Mrs. Gardner burst into tears. She covered her face with her black-bordered handkerchief and her charming figure shook convulsively with her sobs. Her visitor, Dr. Mackenzie, stood with head bowed in silent respect.

Presently Mrs. Gardner recovered herself with an effort, and, gazing appealingly at her visitor through her tear-stained eyes, said:

"Will you pardon me? I know it is very weak of me to give way to my grief like this."

"As I was saying," she finally resumed, "my husband was so dear to me that I cannot bear to think of living in London now he is gone. That is why I am anxious to dispose of my interests there at once. Did you know the late Sir Edward, doctor?"

"I never had the honor of his acquaintance, but I have often heard him lecture, and I have in my library all the books he ever published. I was always a great admirer of his abilities. His discoveries about the circulation of the blood seem to me the most valuable recent contribution to medical science."

"It pleases me to have you say that," said Lady Temple, warming into cordiality at this tribute to her late husband. "I have had many good offers for the practice, but none so far from a man such as my husband would have wished to see succeed him. You are a man after Sir Edward's own heart, and, if you can furnish satisfactory references, I feel confident matters can be arranged to our mutual satisfaction."

From an inner pocket the doctor produced a packet of letters, which he carefully unfolded and handed to Lady Temple.

"Very, very satisfactory," she murmured, after studying them intently. "If my husband were here he would be so gratified to see what an able successor I have found for him. And now as to terms."

The doctor did not seem at all disturbed by this abrupt introduction of monetary considerations. Indeed, he was growing quite merry under the warming influence of her ladyship's bright smiles. These smiles, by the way, were all the more effective because of their background of widow's weeds and tear-stained cheeks.

"Then I may really have the practice?" he asked eagerly.

"Indeed you may," Lady Temple replied. "The price is $25,000, but I do not want to accept that amount or sign the final papers until I get back to London. My solicitors, however, say it will be perfectly satisfactory to give you an option now, provided you are willing to pay just a small amount on the purchase price—say $1,000. Is that agreeable, doctor!"

Agreeable? Indeed it was!

SWINDLING ONE DOCTOR A DAY

The doctor counted out $1,000 in crisp bank notes. Her ladyship produced two copies of an agreement which, she said, her solicitors had prepared, and these they both signed. Then she bade the departing doctor an almost affectionate farewell and gave him the most minute directions about meeting her in London a month later.

The next day I overheard an almost similar interview with a doctor from Glasgow! The only point of difference was that he paid $1,200 for the option instead of $1,000.

There was no necessity for further eavesdropping. I understood now why Lady Temple read all the medical papers and why so many doctors came to see her. No wonder we lived in luxury with some ambitious doctor contributing at least $1,000 every day to our support!

I said nothing of what I had seen or heard, and, although I continued to live with Lady Temple for several months, she never explained her affairs with the doctors. This seems to be a characteristic of all women swindlers—to deceive even their closest friends and never to tell anyone the whole truth about their nefarious schemes. It was from others that I later learned the complete details of this swindle. There really had been a Sir Edward Temple, who was a great London physician.

Mrs. Gardner, learning of his death from the newspapers, familiarized herself with his career from the obituary notices, secured some photographs of him, and began posing as his widow.

Her advertisements in the medical journals did not mention Sir Edward by name, but it was to be inferred that the practice offered for sale was his, because of his recent death and because the announcements were signed "Lady Temple."

Doctors interested were invited to write her at a post office box address. She replied from Nice, where she had "gone for her health," and invited them to come there and see her. What happened to the unfortunate doctors who made the trip I have already told you.

The supply of physicians willing to pay for an option on a London practice seemed inexhaustible and in a few weeks my friend must easily have cleared $20,000. But she began to tire of Nice and invited me to accompany her to London.

When we reached there we went to Claridge's, in Mayfair, and took one of the finest suites in that exclusive hotel. The morning after our arrival she suggested a shopping expedition.

To my amazement there stood at the hotel door waiting for us a splendid carriage drawn by a prancing pair of horses in heavy silver-plated harness.

THERE STOOD A SPLENDID CARRIAGE DRAWN BY A PAIR OF
PRANCING HORSES

On the doors of the carriage was emblazoned a brilliant coat of arms. On the box sat a pompous coachman in livery. A liveried footman stood at attention ready to assist us. I had hard work to believe it wasn't all a dream as I settled back against the soft silken cushions and heard my friend order us driven to Bond street.

We stopped in front of a famous jewelry store—I made ready to alight, but that, it seems, was not the plan. Instead, her ladyship whispered a message to the footman and he went into the store.

Out came the proprietor, a dignified old Englishman. At sight of this splendid equipage with its crests on the door and the two fine ladies inside, he was all bows and smiles.

"It is not customary," he said, rubbing his hands in gleeful anticipation of big sales to come, "to let our trays of diamonds go out of the store, but I shall be glad to arrange it for your ladyship."

A clerk appeared carrying two trays full of diamond necklaces, rings, and other jewelry which Lady Temple had asked to see.

"Have you nothing better than these?" said Lady Temple, rather contemptuously, after a casual glance at them.

The eager clerk hurried back to the store and returned with a tray of more elaborate specimens of the jeweler's art.

Lady Temple leisurely selected a necklace, two rings, and a locket—worth in all more than $5,000.

"Send these to Lady Temple's apartments at Claridge's," she said, "and include them in my bill the first of next month. Doubtless you knew my dear husband, the late Sir Edward"—her voice caught as it always did when she spoke his name—"he had an account here for years."

OUR EXPERIENCE IN LONDON

The clerk smirked his gratitude, promised prompt delivery, and we drove on to a fashionable dressmaker's. There we secured on credit, which had nothing more substantial for its basis than the stolen crest our hired carriage bore, several costly gowns.

This sort of thing went on for two weeks. The magic of my friend's methods opened to us all the treasures of London's finest shops. A never-ending line of messengers brought to Claridge's the most expensive goods of every description—and not a penny of real money was involved in any of the transactions.

I discarded all my old gowns and had to get additional trunks to hold the new ones. Soon I had accumulated three or four times as much jewelry as I could wear at one time. With the prudence for which I was always famous, I put the surplus rings and brooches in a safe deposit box.

All this time you may be sure I felt considerable apprehension. Although I took no active part in these swindling operations, I shared in the plunder, and knew I would be held as an accomplice in case there was trouble.

The trouble came sooner than I expected. We had been "buying" some linens—making our selections, as usual, without leaving our carriage. Just as we were about to drive away the clerk who had taken our order came rushing out.

"Your ladyship's pardon," he stammered, "but would you please step inside the store. The manager thinks there's some mistake—that is, he thought Lady Temple was in Egypt."

I gave a gasp—now we'd be arrested!

But my friend showed not the slightest emotion, except a little annoyance, such as was quite natural under the circumstances to a lady of rank. She calmly walked into the store—and I have never laid eyes on her since.

After waiting an hour I decided she must have escaped by a side entrance. I returned to Claridge's and found she had been there before me. She was gone, bag and baggage—and in a great hurry, as the disorder of the rooms showed.

I lost no time in arranging my own departure and did not feel safe until I was well on my way to New York with my trunks full of more finery than I had ever possessed.

Two or three years later Helen Gardner, alias Lady Temple, was convicted in France for obtaining money under false pretenses. Her prison term brought her to her senses—showed her how foolish it was to waste her life in crime. When she was released she settled down to an honest career and later became the wife of a prosperous merchant.

The account of my experiences with famous women swindlers would not be complete without some mention of the greatest of them all—the notorious Ellen Peck, long known as the "Confidence Queen."

Mrs. Peck's exploits during the many years when she defrauded everybody who came within her reach would fill a book. One swindle would hardly be finished before another would be begun, and often she would have several entirely different schemes under way at once.

She paid her lawyers several fortunes in her persistent efforts to keep out of jail and to retain possession of the property she had stolen. At one time, when she was in her prime, she was defendant in twenty-eight civil and criminal suits.

One of Ellen Peck's many peculiarities was her fondness for practicing her skillful arts on her fellow criminals. She found more satisfaction in cheating a thief out of a ten-dollar bill than in defrauding some banker of $1,000.

Even I, trained in crime from childhood, was not proof against Ellen's wiles. Several times I became her victim as completely as I did Carrie Morse's—and I can vouch for the fact that no shrewder fox ever lived.

Each time she tricked me I would make a solemn vow never to have anything to do with her again. Then along she would come with some story, oh, so plausible!—and I would swallow it as readily as I had the previous one and as much to my sorrow.

Once she actually cheated me out of the very shawl on my back. It was a fine cashmere shawl—one I had secured in Europe at a great bargain.

"Come," said Ellen, "let me have that shawl. I know a rich woman who will give you $500 for it."

"No," I said, grimly, "I don't want to sell it." But Ellen turned her hypnotic eye on me, began her irresistible flow of smooth argument and—got the shawl.

That was the last I saw of her for six months. When I did succeed in running her down she said she had been able to get only $100 for the shawl—and she had left that at home on the sideboard!

Grabbing her by the arm I told her I would not let her go until she gave me what money she had. After considerable argument she emptied $37.50 out of her purse—which was all I ever got for my $500 shawl.

Ellen Peck conceived a very simple scheme of piano swindling, and I was in partnership with her in it. She had been working this swindle alone until she had become known to all the piano dealers. Then she invited me to join her. Here is how we managed it:

I would go to a store and buy a piano on the installment plan, paying five or ten dollars down. The instrument would be delivered at some one of the twenty furnished rooms which Ellen had engaged for just this purpose in various parts of the city.

As soon as the piano was installed at one of these rooms we would promptly advertise it for sale at a greatly reduced price. If the first purchaser did not move the piano at once we would sometimes be able to sell the same instrument to five or six different persons. When we had squeezed as much money as we could out of a piano we would disappear—only to repeat the same trick at another furnished room and with a piano from another store.

It sometimes happened that, when the several persons to whom we had sold a single piano came to claim it, the merchant from whom we had secured it and to whom it still belonged would also put in an appearance. Then there would be the liveliest kind of a squabble, which would have to be settled in the courts.

Crafty Ellen Peck supplied the brains for this enterprise but made me do most of the hard work and gave me only a meager share of the profits. It was a despicable swindle, for the loss did not fall on the dealer, but on the poor families to whom we sold the pianos and who could ill afford the money we took from them. I am thankful to say that I did not long make my living in this mean way.

I hope that Ellen Peck may be alive to read these lines. In her declining years wisdom and charity have doubtless come to her just as they have to me. I feel sure that she shares my sincere repentance for past errors, and that she will give me her hearty endorsement when I say, as I constantly do, that under no circumstances does crime pay.

CHAPTER V

HOW I FACED DEATH, HOW MY HUSBAND WAS SHOT, AND SOME NARROW ESCAPES OF MY COMPANIONS

FROM THE MOMENT WHEN HE COMMITS HIS FIRST CRIME THE PROFESsional criminal never knows what it is to enjoy real peace of mind. His crimes hang over him like the sword of Damocles, and, unless he reforms, he can never be free from the fear of some day being found out and sent away to prison for a long term.

And arrest is not the only thing he has to fear—he is continually face to face with the danger of serious injury or death. Whatever the crime he undertakes, he must run the most desperate risks—he has to stake not only his liberty, but life itself on the narrowest of margins.

The powerful explosive he is using to blow open a safe may go off prematurely, as it did one night when George Mason and I were robbing a bank in Illinois, and leave the robber half dead.

Perhaps an indignant mob may decide to take justice into its own hands by lynching the criminal. This is what happened to one of my comrades in Kentucky. They had the noose around his neck and were all ready to string him up when I arrived in the nick of time to save his life.

Perhaps he will be caught in the act at one of his crimes and shot down like a dog, as my husband, Ned Lyons, was in Connecticut one night. That was the narrowest escape my husband ever had—I saw it with my own eyes, and, if I live to be a hundred, I shall never forget the agony of it all.

At the time of this thrilling adventure the police wanted us so badly for our share in several famous robberies that Ned and I did not dare to undertake any operations in the large cities which usually formed our most profitable fields. So, being in need of ready money, we had decided to take a little trip through some of the smaller towns of New England. The amount of cash to be had from the banks, stores, and post offices in these places was not large, but, on the other hand, it was not hard to get and we thought we ought to be able to spend two or three weeks quite profitably in the nearby towns of Connecticut and Massachusetts.

As my health that summer was not very good and Ned did not want me to take any very active part in the robberies, we invited George Mason to go along with us.

From the start we seemed to be ill-fated. Ned and George succeeded in getting into a bank in Fitchburg, Mass., but were frightened away by a watchman before they had time to open the safe. From the post office in a little village just outside Fitchburg we secured only eight or ten dollars to pay us for our trouble. Quite discouraged and desperately in need of money we went on to Palmer, Mass.

There I scouted around and discovered that the most likely place for us to rob was G. L. Hitchcock's drug store, which was also the village post office. A storm came up to hide the full moon, and this enabled us to make the attempt that very night. It was not the easiest job in the world, for Mr. Hitchcock and his family lived directly above the store and the least noise was sure to rouse them.

HOW WE ROBBED A STORE

Shortly after midnight I took up my position in an alley in the rear of the store to stand guard while Ned and George removed a pane of glass from a cellar window. Through this opening the men squeezed, and presently the dim reflection of their dark lanterns showed me that they had safely reached the store above.

I had been standing there in the rain for nearly twenty minutes when a low rumble from inside the store made me prick up my ears. Just as I was puckering my lips to whistle a shrill warning to my comrades I saw them appear at the back door of the store carrying between them a small iron safe. It was this safe rolling over the floor which I had heard.

The safe was a small affair, but so well made that it had successfully resisted all their efforts to drill it open. Finding it was not too heavy to be carried they had decided to take it outside the town, where they could blow it open without fear of arousing the sleeping village.

We must have made a strange procession as we trudged along through the darkness—the two men partly carrying and partly rolling the safe along, and all of us wading through mud halfway to our knees.

At last we reached a meadow far enough removed from any houses for our purpose. George Mason filled one of the holes he had drilled with black powder and wrapped the safe with some old sacks to protect the fuse from the wet and also to muffle the noise of the explosion.

Ned touched a match to the fuse and we scurried to a safe distance. The charge went off with a dull boom—the shattered door of the safe flew high into the air and landed several yards away.

Waiting a few minutes to make sure that no one in the village had been awakened, we hurried back to get our plunder. There were $350 in cash, a diamond ring, some gold pens, and fifteen or twenty dollars' worth of postage stamps. With the few dollars the boys had taken from the till this made a trifle more than four hundred dollars for our night's work—a pitifully small sum compared with what some of our bank robberies brought us, but enough to support us until we could plan some more ambitious undertaking.

Just as we were dividing our plunder into three equal shares a freight train whistled in the distance.

"George and I will jump on this train," said my husband, giving me a hurried kiss. "It's safer than for the three of us to stick together.

Goodbye—and take care of yourself. We'll meet you in South Windham, Conn., late tonight or early tomorrow." Wet, bedraggled, and so tired that I could have fallen asleep standing up, I groped my way to the railroad station and curled myself up on a bench to snatch what rest I could. Just before daybreak a milk train came along. I boarded this and traveled by a roundabout route to South Windham.

MY HUSBAND IS SHOT

I reached there late in the afternoon and went straight to the post office. This was always the accepted rendezvous for professional criminals when no other place had been agreed upon. Detectives in every city might very profitably spend more of their time watching the post office, for wherever the criminal is he makes a point of calling there at least once every twenty-four hours to keep appointments with his friends or in the hope of running across some acquaintance.

Ned and George were there waiting for me, and mighty glad they were to see me, for they had heard vague rumors of a woman having been arrested on suspicion that she knew something about the Palmer robbery.

The best opportunity the sleepy little town afforded seemed to be a general store run by a man named Johnson. I dropped in there late one evening, and, on the pretext of buying a crochet hook, saw the old proprietor locking the day's receipts—quite a respectable bundle of money—in a ramshackle safe which offered about as much security as a cheese box.

We got everything in readiness to break into the store the following night. It was a foolhardy time for such a job, as there was a bright moon—but we were hungry for money, and one more good haul would supply enough to keep us in comfort until we could lay our plans for some robbery really worthy of our skill.

There was really little I could do to help the men, but I could not bear to be left behind. Just after midnight I stole out of the railroad station, where I had been waiting ostensibly for the night train to New York, and hid myself in the doorway of a livery stable, where I had a good view of the store we were going to rob.

Pretty soon I saw my two comrades come cautiously down the main street from opposite directions. They met underneath a window of the store on the side which was in the dark shadow of a tree.

The window was so high above the ground that my husband had to climb up on George Mason's shoulders to reach it. I could hear the gentle rasp of his jimmy as it worked against the fastenings.

At last he raised the sash gently and stepped into the store. Then he leaned far out across the sill and stretched his brawny arms down toward his companion.

Mason gave a leap, caught hold of Ned's wrists, and, with the agility of a circus performer, swung himself up into the window.

All was as silent as the grave. The only sign of life I could see in the peaceful street were two cats enjoying a nocturnal gambol on a nearby piazza roof. I shivered for fear they might start yowling and awaken somebody to spoil our plans.

Just at that instant one of the cats upset a flower pot which stood at a window opening on the porch roof. To my horror that pot went rolling down the roof with a tremendous clatter, hung suspended for a second on the eaves, then fell to the stone steps with a crash that woke the echoes.

At once the whole town awoke. In every direction I could hear windows being thrown open, children crying, and sleepy voices asking what the trouble was.

At a window directly over the store where my two friends were a night-capped head appeared and a frightened woman screamed, "Help! Burglars!" at the top of her lungs.

That completed the havoc which the playful cats and the flower pot had begun. From every house half-dressed men armed with rifles, shotguns, and all sorts of weapons poured into the street.

All this racket had started too suddenly for me to give Ned and George any warning. I could only crouch farther back in the shadow of my doorway and trust to Providence that the villagers would overlook me in their excitement.

"There goes the burglar now!" someone shouted, and just then I saw my husband dash past my hiding place so close that I could have touched him. He was headed for the open country beyond the railroad tracks and was running faster than I had ever supposed a man of his weight could.

"Stop, or I'll shoot!" yelled an old white-whiskered farmer, who stood, rifle in hand, not a dozen yards away.

But Ned, if he heard the command, made no move to obey. Instead, he only ran all the faster, hunching his head down between his shoulders and zig-zagging back and forth across the road as if to make his bulky form a less favorable target.

The old farmer raised his rifle as deliberately as if he had been aiming at a squirrel instead of a fellow man. Three shots blazed out in rapid succession.

The first shot went wild. At the second my husband stumbled. At the third he threw up his hands and pitched forward headlong in the road.

"We've got him!" the crowd shouted with what seemed to me fiendish glee, and rushed up to where Ned's body lay in a quivering, bloody heap.

I supposed he was dead, but, whether dead or alive, I knew there was nothing I could do to aid him. Nervous and trembling at the awful sight I had seen, I slipped out of town unnoticed.

WHAT CAME OF OUR CRIMES

I saw nothing of George Mason and for months afterward did not know how he had escaped. With better judgment than my husband showed he had remained quietly in the store after the outcry started. He saw the shooting, and, in the confusion which followed, he found little difficulty in getting out of town.

Friends of mine in New London aided me to return to the hospital in Hartford, where Ned had been taken after the shooting. His recovery was slow, for there was a bullet imbedded nine inches deep in his back which the surgeons were unable to remove. As soon as he was able to stand trial he was sentenced to three years in State prison, and, when he had completed this term, he was given three years in Massachusetts for the robbery at Palmer.

This was the result of our crimes in New England—my husband nearly killed and sentenced to six long years in prison. Can you wonder why I have learned the lesson that crime does not pay?

But, to my sorrow, I did not learn the lesson then—no, not for many years after that. With my husband in prison the support of my little ones fell wholly on my shoulders, and I promptly turned to bank robbing as the easiest way I knew of making a living.

My early training under such expert bank robbers as Ned Lyons, Mark Shinburn, and Harry Raymond made me extraordinarily successful in this variety of crime. The cleverest men in the business began to have respect for my judgment and were continually inviting me to take an important part in their risky but very profitable ventures. Soon, as I am going to tell you, my reputation for skill in organizing the most daring robberies and carrying them through without detection had spread even beyond the limits of the underworld.

One day, when I was trying to enjoy the novel experience of living honestly for a few weeks, a distinguished looking gentleman called at my home. He saw my look of incredulity when he announced himself as a bank president and promptly produced a heavy engraved card which confirmed the truth of his statement.

Instantly I was on my guard. In those days my house was the headquarters for all sorts of strange persons—receivers of stolen goods, professional bondsmen, criminal lawyers, escaped prisoners—but I had never before been honored by a visit from a bank president. What on earth could the president of a bank want of a bank robber?

"I understand that you are one of the most successful bank robbers in America," he said without any delay in coming to the point. "I want your advice in a little undertaking I have in mind, and, if possible, your help."

"My advice and help!" I exclaimed, thinking the man must be out of his head.

"That's exactly what I want," he replied coolly. "I want you to tell me how I can have my bank robbed, and, if possible, I want you to take charge of the robbery yourself."

As he explained, he was more than $150,000 short in his accounts. He had taken this amount from the bank within the past year and lost every dollar of it in speculation. He could not return this money and it was only a matter of a few weeks before his embezzlement would be discovered.

Being a man of prominence in his community—a deacon in the church, his wife a society leader, his children in college—running away was out of the question. For months he had been racking his brain for some way of averting the ruin which he had brought upon himself.

The plan he had finally devised for retaining his good name and keeping out of prison was to have his bank robbed. On the night of the robbery he would leave $50,000 in the vault to pay the robbers for their trouble, but, when he came to announce the robbery to the police and the newspapers, he would declare that $200,000 had been taken.

In this way his thefts would be covered up and he could continue to enjoy the respect and confidence of the community where he had always lived.

A BANKER HIRES US TO ROB

I was amazed at the bold ingenuity of this plan and the matter-of-fact way in which he presented it to me. This was the first I had ever heard of a bank being robbed by request of one of its officials. Later I came to know that it is not an uncommon thing for dishonest presidents and cashiers to conceal their thefts by hiring robbers to break into their banks. The difference between what is actually taken in one of these robberies by request and what the police and the newspapers say is taken covers the amount which the embezzling official has lost in Wall Street or some other speculation.

At that time such an idea was so new to me that all sorts of suspicions crowded into my mind. Probably it was a trap for me, I thought, and I positively declined to have anything to do with it.

But the old banker would not take no for an answer. He urged me to think it over and a week later he called again.

WHAT HAPPENED WHEN WE ROBBED A BANK "BY REQUEST"

By this time the fear of the disgrace which threatened him and his family had made him a nervous wreck. He begged so piteously for me to help him save his good name that my womanly sympathies got the better of me and I finally consented.

All my feeling for him, however, did not quite free my mind of the fear that the whole affair might be a trick, and I determined to protect myself and the robbers who would assist me with all the shrewdness I could.

"We must have a written agreement," I said at the very start.

The banker objected to this, fearing, I suppose, that I might use the paper against him later for blackmail. But I insisted that I would not do a thing until I had it.

"If you can't trust me to that extent I can't trust you," I said firmly—and at last he told me to draw up the paper and he would sign it.

According to the contract which I prepared, the banker paid five thousand dollars down and was to pay me an equal amount as soon as I had completed my arrangements and set the date for the robbery. He further agreed that there should be at least $50,000 in cash in the bank vault on the night of our visit.

It was further provided that the banker should cooperate with me and my fellow robbers in every possible way, and that he should do nothing to aid in our arrest or conviction for the crime, which, as was expressly stated, was committed at his suggestion, and not ours. In case the robbery was interrupted before we could get inside the vault the banker was to pay us $25,000 in cash in addition to the $10,000 already advanced.

I agreed to leave no stone unturned to carry out the robbery and promised to return the agreement to the banker as soon as all its provisions had been fulfilled.

All this I set down on paper in as businesslike way as I knew how. It was a document which would have made the poor old banker's ruin even greater than his thievings had done if I had been the sort of woman to break faith with him. With trembling fingers he signed it and counted out $5,000 in bills.

From the banker I had gained a good idea of the bank and the sort of vault we would have to enter. Now, to get some good, reliable men to help me do the job.

Of all the bank burglars in my acquaintance George Mason seemed best fitted for this particular crime. He was a cool, resourceful fellow and had had wide experience in blowing open bank vaults.

George readily agreed to join me, and for the rest of the party he recommended two younger men—Tom Smith and Frank Jones, I will call them, although those were not their names. I do not like to reveal their identity here because they later reformed and led honest lives.

Right here let me say that I never told these three men of my arrangements with the banker or that I was to receive from him $10,000 in addition to what we expected to find in the vault. If they are alive today and read these lines they will learn here for the first time that the bank in Quincy, Ill., which they helped Sophie Lyons rob was robbed by request of its president.

BORING INTO THE BANK VAULT

I sent word to the banker that we were ready and he came to my house and paid me $5,000 more. Then, by different routes, George Mason, the other two robbers and I proceeded to Quincy.

I was the first to arrive. I went to the leading hotel, announced my plan to add a patent medicine laboratory to the town's industries and began to look around for a suitable location for my enterprise. As I believe I mentioned in a previous chapter, this ruse of the patent medicine laboratory was one I had borrowed from my friend, Harry Raymond— he had used it to splendid advantage in his robbery of the Boylston Bank in Boston.

Of course, it was a part of my prearranged plan with the banker that the quarters I should finally find best suited for my purpose would be a room on the second floor of the bank building, directly over the vault we were going to rob.

I made several visits to the bank before I completed my arrangements with the president—partly to carry out my role of the cautious business woman and partly to study the construction of the vault and see where we could best bore our way into it.

By the time the lease was signed the three men who were to be associated with me in the new business arrived. "With their help I secured a quantity of bottles, labels, jars of chemicals, chairs, desks, tables, and other things we would need if we were really making patent medicine.

Among the articles of furniture we moved in was an unusually large oak wardrobe. We removed the bottom from this and placed it over the exact spot in the floor where we planned to dig our opening into the bank vault.

Then, while one of the men and I ostentatiously pasted labels on endless bottles of "Golden Bitters," the other two men crawled into the wardrobe where no chance visitor could see them and day after day continued the work of removing the layers of brick and timber which separated us from the vault. We stored the debris as it accumulated in bags and carried it away every night.

It was a long job and a hard one. The floor timbers were seasoned oak and beneath them were two layers of brick.

In the cramped space inside the wardrobe it was hard to work to the best advantage and, besides, the men never knew just how far they had progressed and were in constant fear that an extra vigorous blow would loosen a big strip of plaster in the ceiling of the bank.

To our disgust we found, after we had passed through the floor itself, that the vault had a sort of false roof composed of short lengths of railroad iron placed irregularly in a setting of mortar and brick. This made our task three days longer than we had expected.

Late one afternoon George Mason cleared away a space which left only a thin layer of lath and plaster between us and the inside of the vault.

There was too much danger of the gaping hole we had dug under the wardrobe being discovered to admit of any further delay. We made our arrangements to rob the bank that very night.

While the rest of the town was going to bed we waited impatiently for it to get late enough for us to lay our hands on the $50,000 which I had every reason to believe was waiting below that thin layer of lath and plaster. Luckily enough the bank's watchman was at a christening party that evening and was not likely to return until the wee small hours. This prevented the necessity of my remaining on guard outside.

Shortly after midnight we turned out our lamps and lighted our dark lanterns. I peered out of the window—the streets were deserted.

George Mason took a small sledge hammer and with one or two well directed blows opened up the hole in the floor wide enough to admit his body. Then he tied one end of a long rope under his arms and we lowered him down into the vault.

MY COMRADE'S NARROW ESCAPE

To the best of my knowledge and belief the cash which had been promised would be found right on the shelves of the vault, and all George would have to do would be to stuff it into his pockets and climb back up the way he had come.

But, whether through intent or an oversight on the president's part, that was not the case. For several minutes we waited breathlessly listening to George as he fumbled around the vault by the light of his dark-lantern. Then we heard him call in a hoarse whisper:

"Sophie, it's just as I was afraid it would be. Every cent of the money is locked up in the small steel safe. I'll have to come back up and get my tools."

It is the custom in big bank vaults to have a small and separate steel safe to put the actual cash into. Leases, documents, account books, and sometimes bonds and stock certificates are kept in the big vault, but money and things of special value are usually locked up in the inside steel compartment.

With some difficulty we hauled him back up. From his bag he selected the drills he thought he would need and from a bottle poured out what seemed to me an extra generous quantity of black powder.

"Be careful and not use too much of that stuff," I called as he disappeared again through the hole. "Ned always said that was your worst failing."

"Don't you worry, Sophie," he replied; "it will take a good big dose to open this safe."

For several minutes we sat there listening to the rasping of his drills against the door of the safe. Just as we felt that tug on the rope which was the signal to haul him up, we saw the flare of his lighted match and heard the sputter of the fuse.

We pulled on the rope for all we were worth but before George 's body was within two feet of the hole in the floor there came a blinding flash, followed by an explosion that shook the building.

Although dazed by the shock and half blinded by the cloud of dust and poisonous fumes which poured up through the hole, we managed to keep our hold on the rope and haul our helpless comrade out of the death trap in which the premature explosion had caught him.

"George!" I called, as we lifted the rope from under his arms. But he never answered and I thought it was only a corpse that we laid gently on the floor. His hair and eyebrows were completely burned off, his face and hands were as black as coal and he was bleeding from an ugly wound in the head.

We forgot the money we were after—we forgot the danger of being caught—in our anxiety for our wounded friend. One of the men brought water while I tried to force a drink of brandy down his throat. It seemed an age before he came to his senses, raised himself on one elbow and roughly pushed me aside.

"It went off too quick for me," he said; "but don't be foolish—I'll be all right in a minute. Look and see if the noise has roused the town."

I looked out—there was not a soul in sight. The bank's thick walls and the fact that it stood at some distance from any other building had evidently prevented the explosion being heard outside.

WE GET THE BANK'S MONEY

Although suffering intense pain George insisted on going back to get the money. It was no easy task, for the vault was full of suffocating smoke. There was no time to lose, as the watchman might return at any minute.

After a few minutes we hauled him up for the third time.

"That charge blew the safe door to splinters, but here's every dollar it contained," he said, handing me several packages of bills.

I counted the money and had hard work to conceal my surprise when I found there was only $30,000. But, as Mason thought himself lucky to escape with his life and, as the other two men seemed well satisfied with the amount, I said nothing.

We started at once for Chicago, where a few days later we divided the spoils. As I had expected, the bank's loss was placed by the newspapers at $200,000. A large reward was offered for the capture of the robbers. I was pleased to note that the president's story of the amount taken and of the complete mystery in which the affair was shrouded seemed to be generally accepted.

After the excitement had died down the bank president came to Detroit to see me. Worry over the possibility of his crime being discovered had shattered his nerves and he was such a poor broken specimen of an old man that I did not have the heart to demand the additional $20,000 which he had promised us. As I tore up our agreement and handed him the pieces, he said:

"My criminal folly has ruined my peace of mind. Thanks to your help, I have saved my family from disgrace, but the worries and nervous strain of my defalcation and the bank robbery have killed me. My doctors say I have heart disease, and have but a few months to live. I wish I had known two years ago what I have since learned—that crime does not pay."

FACING A LYNCHING MOB

The desperate risks every criminal has to run often come through no crime of his own, but through his association with other criminals. Two of the most exciting events in my varied career happened to me through my loyal effort to save the life of my friend, Tom Bigelow, a well-known bank sneak and burglar.

It was in Mount Sterling, Kentucky, that all this happened. I was there on a perfectly legitimate errand and had no idea that any of my criminal friends were in the vicinity.

There was a circus in town that day and the long main street was crowded with sightseers. I had been watching the parade with the rest and was on my way back to the hotel for dinner when I heard someone call my name.

Looking around in surprise I saw Johnny Meaney, a young bank sneak, whom I knew well, pressing his way through the crowd toward me. He was all out of breath and in the greatest agitation.

"Sophie," he whispered in my ear, "they've just caught Tom Bigelow with the bank's money on him and they're going to lynch him."

There was no time to ask him more—before the last word was fairly out of his mouth he had disappeared in the crowd.

As I afterward learned, Tom and Johnny had taken advantage of the excitement created by the circus parade to rob the Mount Sterling Bank. While the cashier was standing upon the counter to see the passing parade, Johnny had crawled in under his legs and taken a bundle of money out of the vault.

He got safely out with his plunder and was just handing it to Tom, who had been waiting in a buggy outside, when the cashier discovered his loss and raised a great outcry. Before Tom had time to stir out of his tracks a hundred willing hands in the crowd had made him a prisoner—then someone started the cry, "Lynch the Yankee robber!" and someone else brought a rope.

In the excitement nimble John Meaney had managed to escape. As he dashed down the street he had chanced to catch sight of me and had passed me the word of our friend's peril.

The crowd was already hurrying in the direction of the square in the center of the town where the courthouse stood and I followed as fast as my legs could carry me.

As I entered the square I could see Tom's familiar form looming above the heads of the yelling mob which surrounded him. He was mounted on a soapbox under an oak tree which stood in front of the courthouse.

I shall never forget how he looked—pale as a sheet, his feet tied with rope, his arms securely bound behind him. He was bareheaded and they had removed his coat and collar in order to adjust the noose which hung around his neck.

Quite plainly, if there was anything I could do to save my friend, it must be done quickly. The mob was loudly clamoring for his life. Already a young man was climbing up the tree in search of a convenient limb over which to throw the end of the rope.

I shuddered to think that, unless I could devise some plan of action, Tom Bigelow's lifeless body would soon be dangling before my eyes.

Summoning every ounce of the nervous energy I possessed I pressed my way through the crowd, screaming frantically:

"That man is my sweetheart! Don't lynch him—oh, please don't lynch him!"

My action took the crowd by surprise—they made a lane for me and pushed me along until finally I stood right at Tom's feet.

HOW I SAVED TOM'S LIFE

I climbed up on the box beside Tom; I threw my arms around his neck, although the feel of that ugly noose against my flesh made me shudder.

"This man is innocent—he is my sweetheart," I kept shouting. "You must let him go."

I hugged Tom Bigelow, I kissed him, I wept over him—I did everything I could imagine a woman doing when the man she loves is about to be hanged before her eyes.

"If you hang him you'll have to hang me, too," I screamed between my heart-rending sobs.

The crowd was amazed. Lynchings were no uncommon occurrence in that region, but nothing like this had ever happened before.

The cooler heads in the crowd began to have their say. "Take that noose off his neck and lock them both up," someone shouted.

The Sheriff put handcuffs on us and led us away. My ruse had succeeded. Tom Bigelow's life was saved!

Tom and I were lodged in jail, indicted by the Grand Jury and held without bail for trial. Of course, I was innocent of any share in the robbery, but, as the authorities believed my story that I was Tom's sweetheart, they thought I must know more about it than I admitted.

It was while we were confined in the jail at Mount Sterling that I had an opportunity to see for myself how it feels to face a desperate lynching mob. That was one of the most horrid nightmares I ever experienced.

One of our fellow inmates in the jail was a man named Murphy Logan, who was awaiting trial for the murder of his father. He was a sullen, weak-minded fellow, who had several killings to his dis-credit. The general opinion was that he belonged in an insane asylum.

In another neighboring cell was a young man named Charlie Steele. He was exceedingly popular in the community. His worst fault was love of liquor and he was in jail for some minor offense which he had committed on one of his sprees. The other prisoners shunned Logan on account of his disagreeable ways, but Steele good naturedly made quite a friend of him and they often played cards together.

In this jail the prisoners were allowed the freedom of the long corridor on which the cells opened. One afternoon Tom Bigelow and I sat just outside my cell trying to devise some way to regain our liberty. Down at the other end of the corridor, Charlie Steele and Murphy Logan were enjoying their usual game of cards.

Suddenly we were startled by a piercing scream. I jumped to my feet, and looked around to see poor Steele lying on the floor with the blood streaming from a long wound in his throat. Over him, glaring like the madman he was, stood Murphy Logan, brandishing in one hand a heavy piece of tin which he had fashioned into a crude sort of dagger.

Forgetful of my own danger, I rushed up and seized Logan's arm, just as he was about to plunge the weapon into Steele's body again. He turned on me, but I managed to keep him from wounding me until Tom and some of the other prisoners came to my assistance.

Steele lived only a few hours. The Sheriff placed the murderer in solitary confinement, and chained him to the floor of his cell. His ravings were something terrible to hear. He continually threatened vengeance on any of his fellow prisoners who would tell how he had slain his friend.

After listening to these threats all night long we were in terror of our lives, and when the inquest was held next day not a single prisoner would admit that he had seen the killing.

"Didn't you see this happen?" the Sheriff asked me.

"No," I lied, "I was in my cell at the time, and don't know anything about how Steele came to his end."

"You lie!" shouted Logan, when he heard this. "If you hadn't inter-fered I would have cut him up worse than I did. I will make you suffer for sticking your nose into my affairs."

The town was in a fever of excitement, and from the windows of our cells we could see excited groups discussing the murder on every corner. Feeling ran particularly high, because the dead man had been so popular in the community while nobody liked Murphy Logan.

Late that night Logan became so exhausted with his ravings that he fell asleep. I was just preparing to try to get some rest myself when I heard the tramp of heavy feet coming up the jail stairs.

By the dim light of the one smoky kerosene lamp I saw a crowd of masked men trooping into the corridor. The leaders carried heavy sledge hammers, and with these, having been unable to make the Sheriff give up his keys, they attacked the iron door of Logan's cell.

It quickly fell to pieces before their sturdy blows. Then they broke the murderer's shackles and dragged him, shrieking curses with every breath, down the stairs and out into the street.

They strung him up to a tree, riddled him with bullets, and left his body hanging there in the moonlight in full view of my cell window. This was too much for my overwrought nerves. I threw myself on my couch and wept. Tom Bigelow did his best to console me, but I could not sleep—my head ached and I trembled in every limb.

About an hour later I heard that ominous tramp of feet again! This time the masked men came straight to the door of my cell.

"Is this where that woman is?" a rough voice called.

I cowered in a corner, too frightened to reply. They pounded the door down just as they had Murphy Logan's. A man seized me by the arm and pulled me out, none too gently.

They were going to lynch me—I was convinced of that. With tears streaming down my cheeks I pleaded, as I never had before, that I was innocent of any crime, and begged to be allowed to go back home to my children.

They took me downstairs into the Sheriff's office, where sat a man who seemed to be the leader of the mob.

"So you tried to save Charlie Steele's life, did you?" he said to me.

Then for the first time it dawned on me that perhaps I was not going to be hanged after all. I told the whole truth about what I had done when I saw Logan waving his dagger over his victim. When I had finished the leader said:

"That's all we want to know, young woman. We liked Charlie Steele, and we like you for what you tried to do for him. Now you're free to get out of town—that's your reward for trying to save poor Charlie. We'll see you safely to the depot."

I was overjoyed. The leader handed me enough money for my traveling expenses and permitted me to go up to Tom's cell and tell him of my good fortune. Before day broke I was on a train for Detroit.

These are only a few of the desperate risks which my husband, my friends, and I were constantly facing during the years when I was active in crime.

If every business man and merchant faced prison, bullets, or a lynching as a necessary risk of trade, would anybody regard business life as attractive?

The incidents from my own experiences give one more illuminative reason why I maintain that crime does not pay!

CHAPTER VI

BEHIND THE SCENES AT A $3,000,000 BURGLARY—THE ROBBERY OF THE MANHATTAN BANK OF NEW YORK

OF COURSE, CRIMES, LIKE BUSINESS OPERATIONS, ARE SOMETIMES BIG AND sometimes small. They vary in importance from the pickpocket's capture of an empty pocketbook to the robbery of a big bank. I will tell you the secrets of the greatest bank robbery in the history of the world—the robbery of $2,758,700 from the vaults of the Manhattan Bank in New York, on the corner of Broadway and Bleecker Street, several years ago.

Every man in that remarkable gang of bank burglars was an associate of mine—I knew them, knew their wives, was in partnership with them. It was an extraordinary enterprise, carefully considered, thoroughly planned, and ably executed; and it yielded nearly $3,000,000 in stolen securities and money. There has never been a bank robbery of such magnitude, either before or since. It was complicated by the difficulty of disposing of the great bundles of valuable bonds, many of which I had to look after.

In my long and varied experiences in the underworld I have never been associated with an enterprise so remarkable in so many different ways as the Manhattan Bank robbery. There were altogether twelve men in this robbery, and every single one of them, with the exception of one, got into trouble through it—one, in fact, was murdered. And here, then, in the biggest, richest robbery of modern times, we learn the lesson that even in a $3,000,000 robbery crime does not pay!

Bank burglars, of course, are constantly casting about for promising fields for their operations, and this great, rich Broadway bank had long been viewed with hungry eyes by Jimmy Hope; Ned Lyons, my husband; and other great professionals. But not only were its vaults of the newest and strongest construction, there was a night watchman awake and active all night in the bank. This watchman was locked in behind the steel gratings of the bank, and Hope and my husband could not figure out any way to get at him and silence him.

It remained for a thief named "Big Jim" Tracy to solve the difficulty. Now the curious part of this is that Tracy was not a bank robber at all. Tracy was a general all-around thief, and specialized more particularly in second-story residence burglaries and highway robberies. Tracy was not even a mechanic and was entirely ignorant of the way to use safe-blowers' tools. But Tracy was ambitious and decided to surprise his acquaintances in the bank burglary line by doing a job which would give him standing among the high-class experts.

STALKING THE WATCHMAN

Tracy had one great advantage—he had been a schoolmate of Patrick Shevelin, one of the bank watchmen. Knowing Shevelin, he was able to renew into intimacy his old acquaintance, and soon broached the subject of the contemplated robbery. Shevelin was a married man, rather proud of the trust reposed in him, and would not consent to have any part in the scheme. If Jimmy Hope or my husband had approached the watchman he would have exposed them to the bank officials, but he had a friendly feeling toward Tracy. Tracy was persistent, held out pictures of a fabulous fortune, and finally gained the watchman's consent.

When all was agreed upon, Tracy decided to get an outfit of burglar's tools and practice up for the job. By this time "Big Jim" was out of money, and he ran up to Troy to pull off a job and put himself in funds. He selected an out-of-town city because he didn't want any trouble in the neighborhood of the scene of the projected bank robbery.

It was in July that Tracy, with a fellow thief, "Mush" Reilly, followed a man named John Buckley out of a bank in Troy, where he had drawn a considerable sum of money. Mr. Buckley got on a street car and Tracy and Reilly crowded in and began work. They were not able to get the man's money without disturbing him, and the result was that Buckley put up a fight. "Big Jim" and "Mush" fought back, but were surrounded by other passengers in the car and arrested. They were tried, convicted, and sent to Clinton Prison for five years.

This misfortune to "Big Jim" Tracy put an end to his designs upon the great Manhattan Bank. But the missionary work which Tracy had already done with Shevelin, the watchman, was destined to bear fruit for others. While "Big Jim" was serving his long sentence in Clinton Prison for the Troy robbery, it became known somehow to Jimmy Hope that Tracy and the watchman of the bank had arrived at an understanding. This was very important news, and Hope at once started in to pick up the thread which had, been so suddenly broken by Tracy's mishap in Troy.

But this was not so easy to accomplish. Shevelin had confidence in his old schoolmate Tracy, but he was afraid of strangers. Jimmy Hope was the Napoleon of bank burglars, and he had in his gang the foremost bank experts of the whole world. Hope found a way to make the acquaintance of Shevelin and he tried every device to win the watchman's confidence. But the shock of "Big Jim" Tracy's long prison sentence had thoroughly frightened the watchman.

With great patience, Hope began a campaign to remove Shevelin's misgivings and make him feel that with such partners he need have no fear. One after another of Hope's great experts were introduced to Shevelin. At dinner one day in a Third Avenue restaurant, Johnny Dobbs was produced, and the exploits of this famous burglar were recounted. Next was introduced George Howard, known as "Western George," and Shevelin was told of this man's extraordinary skill

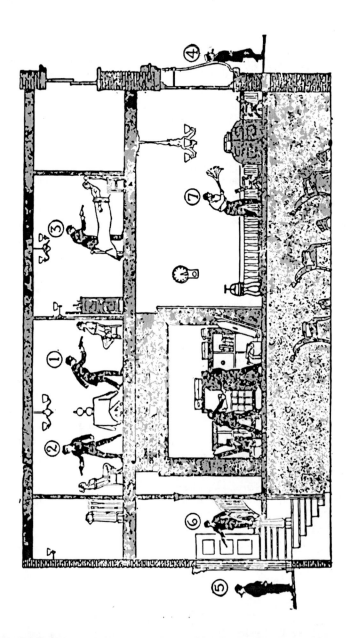

Jimmy Hope, the leader, had considered with minute care every possible avenue of danger, and he placed his men on guard with the precision of a general. Three living human beings were in the building in the rooms over the bank—the janitor, his wife, and his aged mother-in-law. These were quickly taken by surprise, bound, and gagged.

John Nugent (1), with drawn pistol, stood over Werkle, the janitor; Johnny Hope (2), the very promising burglar son of the leader was left in charge of Mrs. Werkle with cocked revolver, while in the next room Eddy Goodey (3) answered for the silence of the trembling old mother.

Outside the bank was more important work to be done. On the Broadway front of the building the venerable Abe Coakley (4) was assigned to duty. On the Bleecker street side George Mason (5) was on post. Just inside the side door, to protect the line of retreat, stood Billy Keely (6), with pistol in hand.

There still remained a delicate matter. In the early hours of the morning it was customary for the old bewhiskered janitor, Werkle, to be seen busy sweeping up the dusting off the desks of the bank clerks. The policeman on post always nodded to Werkle, and if he was not on the job as usual that morning it might arouse suspicion.

In Hope's gang was "Banjo" Pete Emerson, who had been an actor of no mean ability. To him was assigned the job of playing the part of the janitor. With a wig and whiskers made to imitate Werkle, and in shirt sleeves, Emerson (7) busily dusted and re-dusted the desks, keeping close to the street windows, where he could be seen by anybody passing and where he could see and repeat any signals from Coakley and Mason, who were on watch on the sidewalk. "Banjo" Pete played his part so well that the policeman in going his rounds glanced up, saw what he was sure was his friend Werkle dusting the desks, nodded "good morning" and strolled on up Broadway.

Jimmy Hope reserved for himself, Ned Lyons, and Johnny Dobbs the delicate work of blowing the steel safes and taking care of the $3,000,000 of plunder.

on safes and vaults. And then came George Mason and Ned Lyons, whose amazing boldness and quickness with a revolver were already known to Shevelin.

NUGENT, THE POLICEMAN-BREGIAR

A few days later, John Nugent, an able operator and a policeman in good standing, was presented, and a little later on Abe Coakley, the venerable cracksman, was introduced. Finally, the famous "Banjo Pete" Emerson and Billy Kelly and Eddie Goodey were brought to bear on the wavering fears of the watchman.

Shevelin was finally overawed by this powerful aggregation of skill, persistence, and audacity, and consented to join Hope's band of operators. As I look back over that group of burglars, I am sure there was never before gathered together on one enterprise such a galaxy of talent. With such expert skill and such abundant experience as were there represented and all under the able leadership of such a veteran cracksman as Jimmy Hope, surely it was impossible that their enterprise could fail. Shevelin finally realized this, and, as he gave his pledge of help and loyalty, Jimmy Hope shook his hand warmly and said;

"And if we get the stuff, Patrick, your share will be just a quarter of a million dollars. And that's more than you will ever make working as a watchman."

Jimmy Hope now lost no time in setting about his plans for the robbery.

While Shevelin's aid was absolutely necessary, it was only a very short step in itself toward Jimmy Hope's goal, the currency and securities lying in separate steel safes inside the great vault. The entire system of steel plates and locks was the latest, most completely burglar-proof devised. It was universally supposed to be not only burglar-proof but mob-proof. It had been demonstrated theoretically that burglars working undisturbed could not obtain access inside of forty-eight hours. Indeed, it was the very impregnability of the vault which helped in its undoing.

Shevelin could give the band entrance to the building and could bring them to the door of the great vault. But here, in plain view of the street, it would be impossible to study out and assault the combination lock. As the lock could not be studied inside the bank it was evident that the problem must be solved outside.

For this task Hope employed a woman very intimately related to one of the band. While I do not care to give her name, as she is still alive, I may say that she was considered a very attractive woman.

Elegantly dressed she called at the bank and opened an account with the deposit of a few hundred dollars. She made clear to everyone her charming ignorance of banking. She was as amusing as pretty, and before long she was talking to President Schell himself.

It was in fact the president who proudly showed her the massive steel doors and the mighty combination lock which would guard her small deposit. With innocent baby stare she noted the make of the lock and its date.

Possessed of this information, Hope, who was nothing if not thorough, proceeded to buy from the manufacturer a counterpart of the lock. As soon as it arrived the lock was turned over to the inquiring eyes and fingers of George Howard. Ensconced in a little house in a quiet part of Brooklyn, "Western George" made an intimate investigation of the lock's vitals.

Howard undoubtedly was the greatest inventive genius in locks that ever lived, unless, perhaps, Mark Shinburn, a burglar of a similar mechanical turn of mind. He could have made no end of money designing burglar-proof devices, but preferred demonstrating the weakness of the existing ones in a practical way. Hope's confidence in Howard was not misplaced. Within a few days George told the leader he could open the lock by the simple procedure of drilling a small hole just below it and inserting a wire.

Hope watched Howard demonstrate on their own lock and at once planned a prospective tour of the bank to see if the performance could be duplicated on the lock in the Manhattan Bank. If so, they were in sight of their goal.

While the band was waiting for a convenient occasion when Shevelin would be on duty at the bank and could admit them safely to test Howard's grand discovery, a great blow fell upon the whole plan.

It was the mysterious murder of Howard himself. If, as some have suggested, the taking off of Howard was the hand of Providence, I can only point out that the hand was a little bit slow. If Howard had been killed two days earlier, I can't see how the band could have gotten into the vault. Hope, with all his ingenuity and executive ability, was no great mechanical genius on an up-to-date lock, nor was any other member equal to the task.

Howard was on bad terms with several very forceful members of the underworld, at least one of whom was in the dozen who were secretly besieging the Manhattan Bank. While the gang was rejoicing and waiting, a letter came to Howard requesting his immediate presence on important business at a place near Brooklyn.

OPENING THE GREAT VAULT

The following week Howard's body was found in the woods of Yonkers, with a pistol in his hand and a bullet in his breast. The suicide theory was dispelled by finding another bullet in the back of his head. Investigation brought to light that a wagon containing a heap of sacking had been seen driving through the woods and had later returned empty.

Hope and others suspected Johnny Dobbs, of the gang, of doing the shooting, but nothing was ever proved about it.

Dobbs and Hope soon after were let in by Shevelin and they put Howard's theory into practice. They bored a hole about the diameter of a .22-caliber bullet just under the lock, inserted a wire, threw back the tumblers, and had no trouble in getting into the vault.

There stood the safes and from three to six million dollars in money and securities. But this was only a prospecting tour and the two burglars were careful to disturb nothing. Returning, they softly closed the huge door and, Hope manipulating the wire, threw back the tumblers. But Hope lacked the mechanical skill and fine sense of touch possessed by the late lamented Howard, and he pushed one of the tumblers the wrong way. He knew he had made a mistake but was unable to correct it. This meant that the bank employees the next morning would be unable to open the door.

There was nothing to do but fill the hole with putty so that it would not show from the outside and see what the morning would develop. Quite naturally Hope assumed that the lock-tampering would be discovered and his whole plan be ruined. The gang prepared to scatter, but as it turned out they need not have worried.

Sure enough, in the morning the doors refused to respond to the cashier's manipulations. The makers of the lock were sent for, and after infinite labor the door was opened. The experts from the factory who performed the feat were curious to see what had gone wrong with their mechanism. It was in "apple pie" order with the exception of one tumbler which, for no apparent reason, had moved in the wrong direction.

A TIP TO THE POLICE

Jimmy Hope's drill hole, puttied up and nicely-hidden on the outside showed black and conspicuous from the inside. The lock mechanics observed the hole and asked the officers of the bank how the hole came there. They all shook their heads and the subject was dropped. A portly and prosperous looking gentleman who had been standing at the paying teller's window after changing a one hundred dollar bill, heaved a sigh and walked away. It was Jimmy Hope!

"Boys," he said to the band, who were all prepared to abandon the job, "it's a shame to take that money. Those simple souls have found our hole and it doesn't even interest them. They are worrying about a little $20,000 loan on some doubtful security, and here we are within a few inches of from three to six millions."

"Such faith is beautiful," said Johnny Dobbs, with mock piety, "let us pray that it be justified."

Nevertheless the job was postponed for a year on account of information furnished by John Nugent. Nugent, being a member of the New York police force in good standing, was able to keep in close touch with headquarters. He learned that the presence of a dozen of the ablest bank burglars in the world had become known to the police. Not that the police had discovered their presence by detective work, for this happens only in novels or detective plays. When the "sleuth" in actual life gets any real information it is because somebody for fear, hatred, or reward has told him.

As I have said, there was bad feeling in the band and I think someone interested in Howard's death gave the tip. At any rate, the band took pains to scatter, and the various members were careful to record themselves at different cities remote from New York. The New York police were much relieved and promptly forgot the tip that "something big" was to be "pulled off."

Just about a year later Shevelin, who was not by nature intended for a crook, looked up from a drunken doze at a saloon table into the keen eyes of Jimmy Hope. Shevelin had neither the instinctive inclination nor the nervous system which belong to the natural criminal. The bare fact that he was connected with the projected robbery had made a drinking man of him.

He was in debt and in other trouble, and was genuinely pleased to open negotiations again with the able and confidence-inspiring leader. Everything was now in order to go on with the undertaking, there were no dissensions in the gang, therefore the police had no inkling, the bank was smugly confident of their steel fortress, and it only remained to name the hour.

Hope's operations were much embarrassed by the fact that Patrick Shevelin was only a supplementary watchman. Daniel Keely, his brother-in-law, was the regular night watchman, and absolutely honest, as Hope knew, both from his own investigations and from Shevelin's assurances. Shevelin's duty was as day watchman, chiefly during banking hours. The only time when he did not share his watch with either Keely or the equally incorruptible janitor of the building, Louis Werkle, was on Sunday. Therefore, the morning of a beautiful October Sabbath was chosen.

Hope saw that the weak spot of the bank was also the vulnerable point in his own operations, namely, the nervous and somewhat alcoholic Shevelin. Hope decided it would be best for Shevelin to not be on duty at the bank that Sunday, but to arrange with Werkle, the janitor, to take his place.

THE NIGHT BEFORE

Had Shevelin been of sterner stuff, the robbers would have bound and gagged him and left him with a carefully rehearsed tale of a plucky fight against fearful odds to relate to his rescuers. But it was more than probable that Shevelin would betray himself in the inevitable ordeal of hours and hours of tiresome examination. Therefore, it seemed best to have him at home, sick, where he could establish an unshakable alibi and answer, "I don't know" to all questions.

Shevelin admitted the band Saturday night and concealed them in a storeroom in an upper part of the building. There they sat crowded, cramped, and uncomfortable through the entire night. They dared not smoke nor even eat for fear Keely, the regular night watchman, who occasionally poked his nose into the room during his rounds, might notice an unaccustomed smell.

This matter of smell illustrates how carefully Jimmy Hope worked out the minutest details of his plan. He foresaw that ten men packed into a rather small room would, even without food or smoke, make the atmosphere seem close to the nostrils of the watchman familiar with the usual empty smell of the place.

For this reason Hope ordered his men to bathe before the job and wear clean clothing without any scent whatever. No tobacco, drink, or onions passed their lips on Saturday. As a last precaution, at Hope's order, Shevelin broke a bottle of smelly cough medicine on the floor in the presence of his brother-in-law.

As I have said, the regular night watchman was Keely—an honest, incorruptible man. Shevelin was day watchman. Shevelin worked from six in the morning until six at night, when Keely came on duty for the night job.

The janitor of the building, who lived over the bank with his family, was a worthy, honest man, named Werkle. Everybody trusted Werkle, and so it had come about that Werkle was now and then made temporary day or night watchman, whenever Shevelin or Keely were sick or wanted a day off.

Though, as I have said, the genius of "Western George" Howard in discovering a simple and speedy method of opening the lock by inserting a wire through a small hole bored beneath it was the one thing which made Hope's plans feasible, yet, at the last minute, this method became unnecessary.

CONSULTATION IN THE DARK

As if the bank had not done enough in the way of kindness to the burglars by ignoring their little hole, they gave Werkle, the janitor, the numbers of the combination and keys to unlock it. Neither Keely nor Shevelin were trusted to this extent, and Shevelin only learned of the janitor's secret in time to tell Hope the night before the robbery.

This new information was discussed in whispers throughout the night by the gang. Hope had misgivings about using the wire and the hole. The fact that he had failed to return one of the tumblers to its proper place on the previous occasion worried him. It was quite possible he might make a wrong move and, instead of opening the door, lock it irrevocably. In that case it was not to be hoped that the easygoing bank officials would give him a third chance.

On the other hand, forcing the janitor to surrender his keys and reveal the combination had great disadvantages. It meant delay. He might give the wrong set of numbers from fear or loyalty. At any rate he was certain to hesitate. As it proved, time was worth about $100,000 a minute, and ten extra minutes would have doubled the value of the "haul."

Shevelin went home with the understanding that Werkle, the janitor, would take his watch in the morning, when Keely, the night watchman, went off duty. At 10 o'clock, Werkle and his wife went to sleep in their little bedroom above the bank, and Keely made his rounds uneventfully. At 6 o'clock, Sunday morning, Keely waked Werkle, the janitor, and departed by the back door. The closing of the back door was the cue for the gang to take their places and they had no time to lose.

Jimmy Hope and Johnny Dobbs, with Billy Kelly and Eddie Goodey; Johnny Hope, son of Jimmy Hope; Mason; Nugent; and my husband, Ned Lyons, rapidly but stealthily advanced upon the janitor's bedroom. To reach it they had to pass through another bedroom, where slept the aged and feeble-minded mother of Mrs. Werkle.

While gagging and binding the old woman a slight amount of noise was made. Werkle paused in his dressing and remarked that he would step in and see what was doing.

The robbers forestalled him by entering and covering him with their revolvers. They presented a terrifying spectacle, each man wearing a hideous black mask. Rubber shoes on their feet made their steps noiseless. They were received in silent horror.

The tableau was broken by a faint scream from Mrs. Werkle. Instantly cold muzzles were placed to their temples and instant death threatened in return for the slightest sound. Werkle's keys and the combination of the lock were demanded.

Poor Werkle attempted to delay complying, but a few savage prods in his ear with the point of Hope's gun scattered the last thought of resistance. He delivered the keys and told them the combination. Hope had decided at the last moment that as long as he had to tackle the janitor he might as well make him surrender the combination, if possible, and save the trouble and uncertainty of working with the wire and the hole which the bank had obligingly neglected to repair.

Werkle volunteered the objection that the combination numbers would be no use unless they knew how to operate them. Hope inserted a gag in the janitor's mouth and assured him that he need not worry on that score as he was in possession of all the information he needed.

Leaving Johnny Hope and Nugent, the policeman, with cocked pistols watching the bound and gagged janitor and wife and the silent and mysterious Eddy Goodey mounting guard over the helpless old woman, Jimmy Hope and Johnny Dobbs hurried downstairs to the vault, accompanied by Ned Lyons.

Lyons was always a desperate man, who could think and act quickly. In emergency he was governed by instinct, which is quicker than the quickest intellect. In time of trouble, Lyons was always a tower of strength. He would not hesitate at murder, if necessary, and his sudden hand would bolster up a hesitating member of the gang. For this reason he was held in reserve and worked in the vault with Jimmy and Dobbs.

Downstairs, they found, as expected, "Banjo Pete" Emerson in overalls and false whiskers, armed with a feather duster and made up to look exactly like the janitor, Werkle. "Banjo Pete," as his name implies, was a musician, in fact had been a member of a negro minstrel troupe, and was an actor of no mean ability. It was the ability to makeup and act which made Hope cast him for the part of counterfeit janitor. During the entire proceeding, he walked about the front of the bank in full view from the street, dusting the furniture and keeping an eye out for signals from old Abe Coakley, dean of the burglars, who had the responsible position of watching all that went on outside.

FOOLING THE PATROLMAN

A policeman was in sight of the bank during the entire activities, and actually walked up and gazed in the window. "Banjo Pete" looked up from his dusting and waved his hand to the policeman, who thought he recognized his old friend Werkle, nodded "good morning," and then passed on.

Meanwhile, Billy Kelly had taken his place just inside the back door with a pistol and a lead pipe and seated himself on the back stairs, while George Mason was sauntering about outside the door to give warning and prevent interruption from that point.

All these men covered the operations of Jimmy Hope and Johnny Dobbs, who opened the vault door with Werkle's key and combination and fell to work on the steel safes within. There were three, one on either side and one in the back. With the sledge hammer and knife-edged wedges the two burglars spread the crack of one of the safe doors wide enough to force in the necessary explosive. Pausing only long enough to learn from his confederates that the coast was clear, Hope touched it off. A muffled reverberation reached the policeman across the street. He glanced over at the bank.

"Banjo Pete" dropped his duster, crossed to the window, and peered out as if the explosion were from outdoors somewhere, and he were mildly wondering. The policeman resumed his reflections and the work went on. Fifteen minutes later another muffled boom marked the blowing of the second safe.

At this point Hope and Dobbs paused to collect the booty. It was more than they could carry, so half a peck of bonds was passed out to the vigilant Billy Kelly on the back stairs, as much more to the silent Goodey, unwelcome watcher by the bedside of the feeble old woman.

With bulging eyes, Mr. and Mrs. Werkle saw a few bags of gold tossed in to their guardians and pocketed. The gang had been growing richer at the rate of about a hundred thousand dollars a minute for some time.

As Hope and Dobbs returned to attack the third safe, which stood in the rear, there came a threatened interruption. George Mason, outside, gave the signal to Billy Kelly, inside the back door, to be on guard. A milk wagon stopped, the driver descended with a quart of milk, opened the back door, and was about to ascend the stairs with it to deliver to the janitor.

Billy Kelly, on guard on the stairs for just such an emergency, politely informed him that the janitor and his family had gone away and would need no more milk for some time. The milkman replaced the bottle in his wagon and went on, while Hope drove home his wedges.

But now came a serious interruption, the wily old Coakley signaled that the end of their operations had come. It was inevitable that Kohlman, the barber, would soon open up his little shop beneath the bank. This was what Coakley signaled to "Banjo Pete," who called the news to the workers within the vault.

Immediately Hope, Dobbs, and Lyons laid down their tools, put on their coats, stuffed the remainder of the undisturbed plunder inside their clothes, and told the band to quit.

Johnny Hope and Nugent, with a last bloodthirsty threat, left the Werkles. Eddy Goodey pocketed his revolver and joined the group collecting around Billy Kelly on the back stairs, where "Banjo Pete" was getting out of his overalls and pocketing his false whiskers.

George Mason gave the "get away" signal on the outside, and one by one the gang, carrying nearly $3,000,000 in money and securities, mingled with the crowd and vanished.

Coakley, on watch in front, stayed around and waited for further developments.

About ten minutes later the early customers of Kohlman's barber shop heard someone leaping down the stairs from the bank. In burst apparently a madman, half-dressed, his hands handcuffed behind him.

THE JANITOR'S ESCAPE

A gag in his mouth added to his strange appearance. Unable to speak or use his hands, he danced up and down and made growling sounds like a mad dog.

The barber shop emptied itself and Kohlman was not able at once to recognize behind the gag and the jaunty disarray of clothing his old friend Werkle, janitor of the bank.

The gag removed, Werkle was able to blurt out the fact that the bank had been robbed. The policeman across the street was summoned, and with him came Coakley. They heard an amazing and somewhat incoherent tale. The policeman, being rather young and inexperienced, listened open mouthed and did not know what to do.

Coakley, the elderly and rather distinguished looking gentleman, suggested that the story sounded "fishy," and the policeman ought to investigate. He did so. The whole party entered the bank and Coakley was able to note that no telltale clues had been left behind. He observed with regret that, while two of the safes gaped wide open and the third contained several wedges, it was still shut tight.

The policeman held the half-crazed Werkle prisoner and guarded the safe while he sent Coakley to the police station to call out the reserves. This errand Coakley neglected and, instead, looked up Jimmy Hope, who, like most robbers, was leading a double life. He had a wife and children in one part of the city, and in another a fashionable apartment where he was known as Mr. Hopely, a retired capitalist, and had quite a circle of friends, mostly prosperous business men.

From this point luck turned against the band. The tremendous proportions of the robbery caught everyone's imagination. The underworld was as much excited as the police, and talk and speculation would not die down. The neglected hole in the lock came to view again, and it was now appreciated in its full significance.

The polices recollected their tip about Hope and his gang which had come to them at the same time as the discovery of the hole and their suspicions began to grow against some of the real perpetrators. Still, for many weeks, there was not an atom of evidence against any member. Patrick Shevelin, the weak link of the chain, began to feel the pressure.

THE WEAK SPOT

Not only was he a man lacking in the robust nerves essential to a successful criminal, and also one who drank too much, but he was cruelly disappointed as well. He had been led to believe that a quarter of a million dollars in cold cash would be handed to him within a day or two after the robbery. He was going to buy a castle in Ireland and a few other things with the money.

Instead of all this, Hope gave him only $1,200. He explained at the time that this was only his share of the cash stolen, and that the balance of the quarter million would be forthcoming as soon as the bonds and stocks had been converted into cash.

But alas for poor Shevelin. The bonds never were converted and, instead of more money, Hope brought him bad news and actually forced him to return half of the $1,200. He told Shevelin that a bill was being prepared at Washington to compel the issuance of duplicate securities in place of those stolen. This would, of course, make the originals worthless and kill the sale of them and make the robbery a financial failure.

There was truth in Hope's plea, for the bill was actually passed, but it is doubtful if poor Shevelin's $600 was used, as Hope promised, to bribe Senators and Congressmen to obstruct the bill.

The horse being stolen, the bank took pains to lock the barn door. They not only rearranged their leeks and tilled up the hole, but investigated Werkle, Keely, and Shevelin. Finding that Shevelin was drinking and frequenting disreputable places, they were about to discharge him. But the detectives persuaded the bank to retain him for fear discharge might excite the suspicions of the gang.

Detectives shadowed Shevelin night and day. Some of them became acquainted with him under one guise or another. They even became intoxicated with him. On one or two occasions he let slip remarks that he was connected with some big secret affair. One day they saw a bartender get a package from a drawer and hand it to Shevelin, who opened it and took out some bills, and then returned the package. The detective was able to see that the package contained several hundred dollars. This was more than Shevelin, in all probability, would have saved out of his small salary with all his bad habits.

In spite of all this they knew Shevelin was not ripe for arrest. Finally, in a maudlin moment he conveyed the information that he had been the means of making a great achievement possible and that he had been treated very shabbily.

The detectives at once had the bank discharge him on some pretext foreign to the robbery. This added to Shevelin's gloom. When, on top of this, he was arrested, he was quite ripe to confess. That the gang might not become suspicious, he was arrested for intoxication, taken to court the next day, and discharged. As soon as he stepped out of the courtroom he was rearrested, and this procedure was repeated day after day.

Still Shevelin refused to confess until a detective, telling him how much the authorities knew about the case, informed him that all the gang were rich beyond measure except Shevelin.

"What a sucker you were, Pat," he concluded, "to accept a measly $10,000."

Shevelin leaped to his feet and shouted.

"It's a lie. I never got any $10,000, so help me heaven. I never got more than $600 for it."

"I apologize," said the detective, "you are a ten times bigger fool than any one supposed."

Shevelin realized he made a hopelessly damaging confession and within a few hours the police were in possession of the complete details of the case.

THE WATCHMAN'S CONFESSION

For fear anyone should not believe the actual amount that was taken from the bank, I refer you to the following official list of just what we got from the Manhattan Bank as it was announced by the president of the bank:

NOTICE

THE MANHATTAN SAVINGS INSTITUTION was, on the morning of Sunday, October 27, robbed of securities to the amount of $2,747,700, and $11,000 in cash, as follows:

THE STOLEN SECURITIES
- United States 5's of 1881, 8 of $50,000 each, 10 of 10,000 each... $500,000
- United States 6's of 1881, 20 of $10,000 each ... $200,000
- United States 10-40 bonds, 60 of 10,000 each... $600,000
- United States 4 per cents, 30 of $10,000 each... $300,000
- United States 5-20's of July, 1865; 26 of $500 each, 35 of $1,000 each... $48,000
- New York State sinking fund gold 6's, registered. No. 32... $32,000
- New York City Central Park fund stock, certificate No. 724... $22,700
- New York County Court House stock, 6 per cent... $202,000
- New York City, accumulated debt, 7 per cent bonds, two of $100,000 each, and one of $50,000... $250,000
- New York City Improvement stock, 10 certificates of $20,000 each... $200,000
- New York City Revenue Bond, registered... $200,000
- Yonkers City 7 per cent coupon bonds, 118 of $1,000 each... $118,000
- Brooklyn City Water Loan coupon bonds, 25 of $1,000 each... $25,000

- East Chester Town coupon bonds, 50 of $1,000 each...
  $50,000
- Cash... $11,000

  Total amount stolen... $2,758,700
  Charles F. Alford, Secretary.
  Edward Schell, President.

If Hope had found ten minutes more time at his disposal he would have entered the third safe, and, as it happened, come upon almost three million more. However, as it stood, this was the greatest robbery ever achieved, and, as things were, each man of the gang should have been rich.

HUNTING DOWN THE GANG

Now we will see how much crime, even in the most successful case, profited the criminals. In the first place, Tracy was in prison before it happened. "Western George," who solved the lock, was murdered. Patrick Shevelin, the watchman, received, instead of the quarter of a million, actually $1,200 in cash. Within a few days Jimmy Hope took half of this back again on the plea that it was needed at Washington to buy off legislators who were to pass a bill through Congress ordering the issue of duplicates in place of the stolen securities. As an actual fact, all Shevelin ever profited from this robbery was $600.

Jimmy Hope and John D. Grady, the fence, quarreled over the disposition of the bonds and stocks, which Hope spirited away and hid in the Middle West. The dissension spread to other members of the gang and the underworld began to hear details of the robbery.

Hope failed in his efforts to prevent the passage of the bill canceling the stolen securities, and then came the final blow—the confession of Shevelin.

Hope was caught in San Francisco, his son, Johnny Hope, was captured in Philadelphia while trying to dispose of some of the bonds—and one after another the gang was run down.

Considered from a technical viewpoint, this robbery was the most Napoleonic feat ever achieved. My husband, Ned Lyons, said Hope ought to have managed without the aid of Shevelin or, if his aid was absolutely necessary, he should have been killed. This point of view regarding murder is one of the distinguishing differences between my husband and Jimmy Hope.

And thus we find that the greatest bank robbery in the history of the world, which enlisted the time, brains, and special skill of a dozen able men over a long period of time, resulted in failure to dispose of the valuable securities, and landed sooner or later most of the operators in prison. If an enterprise of such magnitude, successfully accomplished, was not worthwhile, then surely crime does not pay!

CHAPTER VII

BANK BURGLARS WHO DISGUISED THEMSELVES AS POLICEMEN, AND OTHER INGENIOUS SCHEMES USED BY THIEVES IN BOLD ATTEMPTS TO GET THEIR PLUNDER

No honest man can accumulate a million dollars without constant industry, self-denial, perseverance, and ability.

The same is true of the professional criminal. In addition, he must possess ingenuity, tact, and resourcefulness of a high order.

I have mentioned a number of professional criminals who, in the course of their careers, obtained over a million dollars apiece. Although these men accumulated vast fortunes, there was not a single one of them who really derived any lasting benefit out of his ill-gotten gains. Many of them spent a large portion of their lives in jail. Behind prison walls, their buried loot availed them nothing. Others dissipated their fortunes almost as rapidly as they made them and their last years were spent in poverty. Some of them died violent deaths.

Yet every one of these men, as I have intimated, possessed valuable qualities which, had they been put to a legitimate use, would undoubtedly have brought them wealth without any of the penalties incident to a life of crime. Living honestly they might not have accumulated millions, but their skill, ingenuity, and perseverance would undoubtedly have netted them large incomes, and they might have enjoyed the peace of mind which none but the law-abiding can know.

Without the ability which these men possessed, it would be useless for anyone to hope to achieve the "success" which attended their criminal operations. But anyone possessing their ability would be most ill-advised to attempt to follow in their footsteps when their careers have so clearly demonstrated that crime cannot pay. Whereas, if properly applied, such ability must inevitably bring success.

I intend to give you some idea of the skill and resourcefulness these men possessed by referring in detail to some of their more remarkable exploits.

In the course of a criminal career covering some forty years, Harry Raymond, all-round burglar, committed several hundred important burglaries. It was he who stole the famous Gainsborough painting, as I have previously related. The magnitude of his crimes will be indicated by the fact that his booty aggregated between two and three million dollars. Yet, despite the number and importance of this man's offenses, he was caught only once in the whole forty years, and then through the carelessness of an accomplice. No better proof of the judgment and resourcefulness of a professional criminal could be presented than such a record as that.

His robbery of the Cape Town Post Office will illustrate this point more concretely.

His first step was to cultivate the friendship of the Postmaster of the Cape Town Post Office. He went at it very systematically and patiently, but at the end of two or three months he had made such progress that he readily found an opportunity to get temporary possession of the post office keys. That was all that was necessary. He made a wax impression of them and put the keys back without arousing any suspicion.

His next step was to prepare three parcels addressed to himself, and mailed them by registered mail from out of town. He came in on the same train with the packages. He waited until the registered mail sacks had been delivered to the Postmaster and locked up for the night, and then, just as his friend, the Postmaster, was leaving for the day, he stopped hurriedly into the post office and explained that it was of great importance for him to get that night certain packages he understood were arriving by that day's registered mail. The Postmaster readily consented and went back into the office with the burglar. He opened the safe and ascertained that the packages Raymond had described were there, and while he was making certain entries in his book, Raymond succeeded in making wax impressions of the keys to the safe.

Raymond now had wax impressions of the keys to the post office itself and of the keys in which the registered mail and other valuables were kept.

Making the keys from the impressions was not a very difficult task, although it required many subsequent visits to the post office and the exercise of a considerable amount of patience before the keys were properly fitted. Then Raymond waited for the diamonds to come from the mines, his plan to get them into the post office safe having been very carefully thought out.

At one stage of the trip the diamond coach had to make, it was necessary for it to cross a river. This was accomplished by means of a ferry which was operated by a wire-rope cable. Raymond decided to spoil this plan. Before the coach arrived at the ferry he succeeded in severing the wire cable. There was a strong current running and the ferryboat naturally drifted down the stream.

When the coach arrived at the river, there was no ferryboat to take it across, and there was no other means of fording the stream. As I have mentioned, the schedule of the coach had been arranged so that it would reach the docks just in time to catch the steamer for England. The delay at the river resulted, as Raymond had known it would, in the coach missing the steamer, and the next steamer wouldn't sail for a week. In the meanwhile, the diamonds were deposited in the post office safe.

It was an easy matter for Raymond to get into the post office the following night, and the keys he had made gave him access to the safe.

The diamonds and other valuables he had planned so cleverly to get were worth $500,000. He abstracted them all and buried them.

Instead of fleeing the country with his booty, his prudence dictated that he was safest right there, and he remained there for months. Subsequently, he disposed of the stolen diamonds in London, but he was blackmailed out of a large portion of the proceeds by the accomplice with whom he had made his first attempt to rob the diamond coach, and who at once concluded when he heard of the successful robbery that it was Raymond who had committed it.

Although it netted the burglars only $100,000, the robbery of the Kensington Savings Bank of Philadelphia was one of the most cleverly arranged crimes of modern times.

The theft was committed by a band of the most notorious bank burglars of the time, including Tom McCormack, Big John Casey, Joe Howard, Jimmy Hope, Worcester Sam, George Bliss, and Johnny Dobbs, No more competent crew of safe cracksmen could possibly have been gotten together.

On the day these burglars planned to rob the bank, the president received information that the crime was contemplated and would probably be committed that night or the night following.

This information came apparently from the Philadelphia Chief of Police, the messenger stating that the Chief would send down half a dozen uniformed men that afternoon, who were to be locked in the bank that night. The president was told to keep the information to himself as it was desired to catch the burglars red-handed, and it was feared that word might reach them of the plan to trap them and they would be scared off.

That afternoon half a dozen uniformed policemen called at the bank shortly before the closing hour. They were called into the office of the president and introduced to the bank's two watchmen. After the bank was closed the six men were secreted in different parts of the building and the watchmen were told to obey whatever orders the policemen might give.

Nothing happened until about midnight, when some of the policemen came out of their hiding places and suggested to one of the watchmen

SOON AFTER MIDNIGHT A STRANGE SCENE WAS ENACTED

that it might be a good idea to send out for some beer. One of the policemen volunteered to take off his uniform, but changed his mind, saying that it would perhaps be safer for one of the watchmen to go.

"If the burglars see one of you fellows going out of the building," he said to the watchmen, "they will suspect nothing, but if they see a strange face leaving the bank at this hour they will know there is something unusual going on." The watchmen agreed.

No sooner had the watchman left the building than one of the policemen raised his nightstick and brought it down with all his might on the head of the other watchman. The man dropped to the floor like a log. He was quickly bound and gagged and taken inside the cashier's cage.

A few minutes later the other watchman returned with the beer, and as he set foot in the room where the policemen were congregated he was accorded the same treatment.

The watchmen out of the way, the six policemen made their way to the bank safe and there a remarkable scene was enacted. Attired in the regulation uniform of the city police, with helmets, shields, and nightsticks of the official style, the six "policemen" proceeded to break into the bank safe. As their work progressed, some of the men removed their hats and loosened their heavy coats, but there was nothing to indicate to anyone who might have witnessed this remarkable piece of work that the men engaged in the cracking of the safe were not genuine policemen. As a matter of fact, of course, they were six of the cleverest bank burglars in the business.

When the safe was blown and the bank's funds, amounting to some $100,000, removed, the "policemen" buttoned up their uniforms, put on their hats and, opening the front doors of the bank with the keys they took from the unconscious watchmen, they boldly marched in single file into the public street.

In planning out a bank robbery, or, indeed, any kind of robbery, a great deal of time must be given over to study of the situation so that when the day of the robbery comes the burglars will know just what to do and be able to do it promptly. Oftentimes it is necessary to wear a disguise so as to more surely carry out the prearranged plans.

I remember once disguising myself as a Quaker farmer's wife when we did a job in the section of Pennsylvania where the Quakers abound. We had been over the territory very carefully and picked out a bank where a considerable amount of money was on display, scattered around on the different counters of the bank, and we decided that we could go into that bank in broad daylight and get most of the cash.

For several weeks we had studied the methods in vogue in the bank and knew pretty accurately where the cashier and other employees would be at certain hours, and which hour would be the most favorable for our work.

There were four of us working on this particular robbery, and it was decided that I should disguise myself as a Quaker woman and pass the bank at a certain hour. I went around the town for several days studying the costumes of the women and finally rigged myself out in the typical Quaker housewife style.

I purchased a small milk can and, as its newness might attract attention, I rubbed the can with dirt until it took on a time-worn appearance. Then I secured one of the common baskets carried very often by the women who go to market to dispose of small lots of vegetables. For several days my pals and myself rehearsed the work we had to do so that when the time of action came we were perfect in our parts.

We had found out from our daily observations of the bank that the cashier, who was a good deal of a dandy, went out every day at half past twelve and returned about 1 o'clock. Several of the other clerks in the bank went out for their lunch at the same time. At fifteen minutes to one there were fewer clerks in the bank than at any other period of the day, and if we were to do our work at all it must be accomplished at that time.

There was only one drawback to this arrangement—the cashier occasionally came back at five or ten minutes to one, and we could not be certain that he would stay out the full half hour on the day we operated. If he came back before 1 o'clock our scheme would be frustrated and we would probably be arrested. So it was decided that I should lay outside the bank and intercept the cashier if he should happen along before my pals made their getaway from the bank.

On the day of the robbery we were near the bank at half past twelve, and waited till a quarter of one, when we saw several other clerks go out. Then the rest of my band hastened into the bank, and I kept my eyes fixed on the direction in which the cashier usually came. The robbers who went into the bank had a number of little formalities to get over before it was possible to grab the money, and this took time.

They had been inside nearly ten minutes when I spied the cashier walking up the street toward the bank. As luck would have it, he was getting back five minutes ahead of his usual time. I strolled leisurely to meet him, dressed up, of course, as the Quaker housewife, with my basket full of vegetables and can of milk on my arm.

The cashier and I came together in the middle of the block, about a hundred feet from the bank. I accosted him and asked for some ficti-tious address, in a broken English kind of lingo, which he could not at first understand. He was a very polite young man, and, of course, stopped to help me out of my little difficulty.

While I was engaging the cashier in this fashion, I kept my eyes rambling to the bank to see if my pals were getting away, for if the cashier had gone down at that moment he would see them in the act of robbing, and all would be lost.

After holding the cashier for a minute or two, he became impatient at my unintelligible talk and said he was sorry he could not help me and would have to be going. Now, under no circumstances could I permit that cashier to leave then. If necessary I would have grabbed him about the neck and held him by force until my companions escaped. But a better scheme than this suggested itself; I deliberately spilled the can of milk over the cashier's clothes, doing it, of course, in an apparently innocent way.

The nice white milk settled all over the young man's vest and coat, and he looked a sorry sight indeed. He was exasperated at my awkwardness, as he called it, and took out his handkerchief to wipe off the milk, and I, full of sympathy for his deplorable plight, also took out my handkerchief and gave my assistance. While we were trying to get rid of the milk I saw the robbers hurry out of the bank and walk rapidly up the street. Then I knew they had gotten the cash, and it was no longer necessary for me to detain the cashier. I mumbled my apologies to the poor, milk-bespattered cashier, and then hurried off down the street.

I went into a doorway—which I had picked out in advance, of course—and took off my Quaker disguise. Under the disguise I had on my regular clothes. I left the Quaker outfit, milk can and all, in this strange doorway and then hustled off to meet my pals at the rendezvous previously agreed upon.

We divided the money—we had obtained $90,000—and stayed in the town a few days.

In the papers the next morning there was a big account of the robbery, and the additional statement that the robbers had overlooked another package of money containing $150,000. We were shocked by this piece of information, and the poor robber whose duty it was to collect the money in the bank was roundly upbraided for getting a miserable ninety thousand when he could also have taken the

$150,000 if he had not been such a bungler. He swore by every deity that the papers were wrong, for he had searched very carefully and there was no other money in sight when he left the place. However, we could never forgive this chap for his oversight, because we believed the papers had the thing right, and we disputed about the matter so much that the gang, or "party," as we of the criminal fraternity call it, had to be disbanded, and we went our separate ways, good friends, of course, but no longer co-workers.

It is the custom among bank robbers to demand that each member of a party do his work properly. If any one of them makes a failure, or does not come up to expectations, he is discharged from the party. The method of discharging a member is peculiar. The leader will say to him: "When are you going home, Jack?" and he will hand him some money. "When are you going home?" means we don't want you with us anymore. I might say, in concluding this experience, that one of the men who took part in this robbery is now living in Philadelphia and highly respected. He long since gave up his criminal associations and went into business for himself and has made a great deal of money by his own honest efforts.

The other man died in prison. His was the fate of many another professional criminal. He had gambled away most of the money he secured from his illegal trade and, in addition, he served twenty years of his life behind prison walls.

Not even the cleverest men in the business have profited by their skill. They may prosper for a brief hour, but in the end they are forced to the conclusion that crime does not pay!

CHAPTER VIII

PROMOTERS OF CRIME—PEOPLE WHO PLAN ROBBERIES AND ACT AS "BACKERS" FOR PROFESSIONAL CRIMINALS: THE EXTRAORDINARY "MOTHER" MANDELBAUM, "QUEEN OF THE THIEVES" AND GRADY, WHO HAD HALF A DOZEN GANGS OF CRACKSMEN WORKING FOR HIM

IF THERE IS ANY ONE FAMILIAR ADAGE THAT FITS EVERY CRIMINAL IN the underworld it is "Easy come, easy go." Surely there is a curse on stolen money. More than once in my former life I have received $50,000 as my share in a Sunday morning bank burglary—and by the next Saturday night not even a five-dollar bill remained.

Professional thieves are rich one day and poor the next. The fact that more money is always to be had without the hard labor which brings honest reward makes thieves as improvident as children. All

"MOTHER" MANDELBAUM'S FAKE CHIMNEY AND SECRET HIDING
PLACE FOR STOLEN JEWELS

thieves are gamblers—scarcely in all my acquaintances can I recall even one exception. Sometimes the entire proceeds of a robbery are lost in a gambling house within twenty-four hours after the crime.

And this is how it has come about that all over the world, in every big city, there are "backers" of thieves: men, and sometimes women, who take the stolen goods off their hands, find hiding places for criminals who are being pursued, advance money to them when they are out of funds, and even pay the expenses of their families when the burglars get into prison.

Some of these friends of thieves are really promoters of criminal enterprises. They name the banks and jewelry shops that are to be robbed and select the residences of wealthy persons that are to be entered. They are like the backers of theatrical enterprises who put up the money for the necessary expenses and advance the salaries of the actors; they are like the promoters in the mining world who pay for the tools, the pack animals, and who "grub-stake" the miners to outfit them on prospecting tours in the mountains.

QUEEN OF THE THIEVES

Curiously enough the greatest crime promoter of modern times was a New York woman, "Mother" Mandelbaum. Alas! I knew her well—too well. A hundred, yes, perhaps near five hundred transactions I have had with her, little and big. Many were entirely on my own account, oftentimes I dealt with her in behalf of thieves who were in hiding or in need of help or were in jail.

Nobody anywhere did such a wholesale business in stolen goods or had such valuable associations among big criminals. "Mother" Mandelbaum, of course, cracked no safes, she did not risk her skin in house burglaries, her fat hand was never caught in anybody's pocket, no policeman's bullet was ever sent after her fleeing figure. Here, then, we have a dealer in crime pretty shrewdly protected from the dangers that beset criminals. And yet I shall once again prove to my readers and from this very woman who was the uncrowned "Queen of the Thieves," rich, powerful, and protected by the police—from this very "Mother" Mandelbaum I shall again show that crime does not pay!

But was this woman exceptionally unlucky? No. I will recount to you also the career of John D. Grady, her very remarkable rival in the same field of criminal promotion—the man who financed the great $3,000,000 Manhattan Bank robbery and had the famous Jimmy Hope and his band of expert cracksmen in his employ. From Grady I will also prove the great moral truth that surely crime does not pay!

"Mother" Mandelbaum's real name was Mrs. William Mandelbaum. She was born in Germany of poor but respectable parentage. As a young woman she arrived in America without a friend or relative. But her coarse, heavy features, powerful physique, and penetrating eye were sufficient protection and chaperone for anyone. It is not likely that anyone ever forced unwelcome attentions on this particular immigrant.

Arrived in New York, she was compelled to pawn one or two gold trinkets while looking for work. This brought her in touch with the flourishing pawnshop business.

ENCOURAGING PICKPOCKETS

The pawn shops were practically unregulated by law in those days and the German girl's painful experience as a customer, instead of making her angry, impressed her with great admiration. There was a field for an ambitious person, and if ambition is a virtue none was ever more virtuous in that particular than "Mother."

But how to enter this profitable industry was the question. To be a pawnbroker has always required capital. That is, it always has for anyone but this woman, who had none. She made a hurried survey of the pawn shops along the Bowery and elsewhere, and among others noticed the place of one William Mandelbaum.

William was unmarried, rather weak willed for a man of his calling, lazy, and afflicted with chronic dyspepsia. He cooked his own meals over a kerosene lamp, which was undoubtedly the cause of his indigestion. "Mother" Mandelbaum introduced herself as Fredericka Goldberg, and offered to cook and tend store at nominal wages.

The "nominal wages" item secured her the position and the cooking made her firm in it. Within a week, William's digestion was better than he could ever remember since boyhood; he had gained seven pounds in weight and business was growing beautifully—all on account of the capable Fredericka.

At the end of the week, William and Fredericka had a business talk. Fredericka didn't want an increase in wages. She didn't want any wages at all. It was partnership or nothing. William ate one meal cooked by himself and then surrendered. Within a few weeks they were married. Mrs. Mandelbaum forever afterward was the head of the house of Mandelbaum.

Among her customers Mrs. Mandelbaum noticed an occasional one who would hurry in and get what he could on a miscellany of watches and small pieces of jewelry. These hasty, furtive young men and boys took what they could get and showed little disposition to haggle. Also, they never returned to redeem their pledges.

The new head of the house encouraged these customers, who were, of course, pickpockets. At first, through ignorance, and later, as a matter of policy, Mrs. Mandelbaum was more liberal in her terms than was customary. Some pawn-brokers would not accept anything from a pickpocket if they knew it. The others took advantage of the pickpocket's peril of the law to drive the hardest possible terms.

It was not long before Mandelbaum's had the lion's share of the pickpocket business. One who disposes of stolen goods is known as a "fence," and Mrs. Mandelbaum soon became one of the most important "fences" for pickpockets in the city.

As the pawn shop grew more and more notorious, the weight of the police grew heavier and heavier on the proprietress. She dealt less liberally with pickpockets than before. She squeezed them to the last notch, but they still remained her customers for she was no harder than the other fences.

In order to meet the ever increasing blackmail of the police, Mrs. Mandelbaum found it necessary to steadily enlarge her business. Carefully she developed a system for scattering her stock so that her New York headquarters never contained a very large stock of stolen goods. She kept men busy melting down gold and silver and disguising jewelry and others ferreting out supposedly honest merchants who were willing to buy her wares and ask no questions.

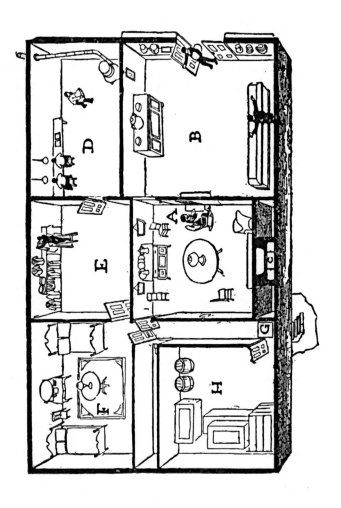

If ever anybody lived in the proverbial "glass house," surely it was "Mother" Mandelbaum—and she knew it. Her establishment was ostensibly a general store and a pawnbroker's office, which she maintained in the front room (B), but Mrs. Mandelbaum also dealt in stolen goods of all kinds and planned robberies with thieves, and often sheltered, protected, and hid thieves in times of trouble.

"Mother" Mandelbaum was never seen in the front room (B), where a clerk was always kept on guard. She kept out of reach behind the window with the steel grating (A). Her false chimney and secret dumb-waiter arrangement was at the point (C). In the room (D) "Mother" Mandelbaum kept two or three employees busy removing stolen jewels from their settings and engraving designs to cover up and hide monograms and identification marks on watches, jewelry, and silverware.

In the room (E) were kept bulky articles and stolen goods, such as fur coats, etc. Here, too, the price tags, factory numbers and other marks were always removed from stolen furs, laces, and silks. The room (F) contained beds where thieves were lodged when occasion demanded. The room (H) was a store room, where crates and cases of stolen goods were packed up for shipment to her customers. At the end of the passageway leading to the room (H) was a secret trap door (G). In case of a raid by the police, and if her front and back doors were guarded by detectives, she could use the trap door (G) to let thieves escape down through a hole in the basement wall, which led up into the house next door, which "Mother" Mandelbaum also owned under another name.

It must always be borne in mind in these articles that crime cannot be carried on by individuals. It requires an elaborate permanent organization. While the individual operators, from pickpockets to bank burglars, come and go, working from coast to coast, they must be affiliated with some permanent substantial person who is in touch with the police. Such a permanent head was "Mother" Mandelbaum.

The field of usefulness to thieves of the big "fences" like "Mother" Mandelbaum and Grady are infinite. Suppose you are a burglar and last night's labors resulted mostly in jewelry and silverware, you would have neither the time nor the plant to melt down the silver and disguise or unset the stones. "Mother" Mandelbaum would attend to all that for you on about a 75 per cent commission.

This wonderful woman kept certain persons busy on salary melting down silver. Others worked steadily altering, unsetting, and otherwise disguising jewelry.

What would you do with a stolen watch which bore, deeply engraved on the back, the name and address of its rightful owner? You might melt down the case and get a little something for the works, but "Mother" would do better. She would turn it over to one of her engravers who would rapidly and not inartistically engrave a little scene or decoration on the watch case, completely masking the name and address.

A stolen automobile is the worst kind of a "white elephant" on your hands unless you know where to take it. Every city has its plants where a stolen car is quickly made over, usually into a taxicab, and so well disguised that its former owner may pay for a ride in it without suspicion.

The force of artisans and mechanics employed on the fruits of burglaries and pocket picking is several thousand in a city the size of New York or Chicago.

All burglars and thieves are busy with their own enterprises, and have no time to look after all these matters. Somebody there must be who will organize these first aids to the captured criminals—the "squarers of squealers," the lawyers, the men to provide bail, etc. Such a one was "Mother" Mandelbaum.

Hacks, taxicabs, express wagons, and even moving vans must be readily available. Peddlers are extremely useful. They prowl about wherever they please and act as advance men for the burglars. Keeping peddlers and tramps off your premises is one of the best forms of burglar insurance.

The army of enemies of society must have its general, and I believe that probably the greatest of them all was "Mother" Mandelbaum.

ROBBING TIFFANY

Of all the stolen things brought into her shop, Mrs. Mandelbaum preferred diamonds. She rapidly became an expert on stones and they presented few difficulties.

A stone once outside its setting usually bears no "earmarks" by which it can be identified. Nothing is so easily hidden nor so imperishable as a diamond, and, as everyone knows, they have an unfailing market. She exhorted her pickpocket customers to specialize on stickpins, and doubtless they did their best to please her.

While pickpockets are "pickers," they cannot always be choosers, and the percentage of diamonds remained disappointingly low. This interest in diamonds brought the "fence" to visit Tiffany's several times. She stole nothing; in fact, I am sure "Mother" never stole anything in her life. But it cost her nothing to examine and admire the beautiful stones, and during one of her visits she was struck with an ingenious idea which marked the second step in her career. She planned a robbery.

In the rear of the Mandelbaum store a consultation was held between the proprietress, a confidence man known as "Swell" Robinson, and a shoplifter, just arrived from Chicago, by the name of Mary Wallenstein.

Robinson, as his name would indicate, was a man of good clothes and presence. He walked into Tiffany's, went to the diamond counter, and spent a long time examining the big stones. After about twenty minutes of questioning he was unable to make up his mind and decided to think the matter over and return later.

One of the stones valued at about $8,000 was missing, and the clerk very apologetically asked Robinson to wait a moment while he searched for it. A dozen employees hunted and counted the stones while Robinson grew more and more indignant at the evident suspicion that he had taken the stone.

At last things came to a head and Robinson was led to a room and searched.

Nothing was found and the store, knowing they had been somehow robbed, were compelled to let him go. The excitement had not quieted down when Mary appeared.

She went to the same counter and stood exactly where Robinson had been. She examined one or two small diamonds and, like Robinson, she concluded to go home and think it over. There was no objection made, for there was nothing missing this time. An hour later she handed the $8,000 gem to "Mother" Mandelbaum.

The following morning the man who polished the counters at Tiffany's found a piece of chewing gum wedged underneath the counter where nobody would see it. Inspection of the gum revealed the impression of the facets of a diamond of the general size of the missing stone. Then everyone understood. The man had placed the gum beneath the counter when he came in. At his first opportunity he stuck the diamond in it. The girl coming in later had only to feel along the counter and remove the gem to make the theft complete.

This first robbery planned by "Mother" Mandelbaum was so delightfully successful that the pickpocket industry seemed slow by comparison. The chewing gum trick could not be worked again, because the jewelers' association had notified all its members of the new scheme. It was a short step from jewel-stealing to sneak-thief operations in banks. Sneak thieves and confidence men began to frequent the back rooms of the Mandelbaum establishment. It became a clearing house for crimes of larceny—big and small.

Many able and successful burglars are unimaginative, and, left to their own devices, would never discover anything to rob. These earnest but unimaginative souls hung about the premises as if it were an employment agency waiting for the "boss" to find a job suited to their particular talents.

DRY GOODS STORE THIEVES

On the other hand, timid but shrewd and observant persons frequently saw chances to steal which they dared not undertake. Servants of wealthy New York families learned that "Mother" Mandelbaum paid well for tips and plans of houses.

Next came employees of wholesale and retail dry goods houses.

To handle bales of silk and woolen, furs, blankets, and other bulky but valuable merchandise presented new problems. To meet these Mrs. Mandelbaum moved her establishment to larger quarters. She retained the pawnbroking department, but added a miscellaneous store, in which she carried for sale most all the articles found in a country store.

She was now the mother of three children, two daughters and a son—Julius. One of the daughters married a Twelfth Ward Tammany politician. This political alliance was extremely valuable. It made the police more moderate in their extortion for immunity, and was the means of obtaining pardons, light sentences, and general miscarriage of justice on the part of judges.

I shall never forget the atmosphere of "Mother" Mandelbaum's place on the corner of Clinton and Rivington Streets. In the front was the general store, innocent enough in appearance; and, in fact, the goods were only part stolen, and these of such a character that they could not possibly be identified.

"Mother" Mandelbaum led a life which left her open to many dangers from many different directions. Every member of the underworld knew that stolen goods of great value were constantly coming into her resort and from time to time schemes were devised to plunder the famous old "fence."

Mrs. Mandelbaum always sat inside of a window which was protected by strong steel slats. The door to the room was of heavy oak. It was impossible, thus protected, for anybody to make a sudden rush and catch "Mother" Mandelbaum off her guard.

But, realizing that thieves might at any moment raid her establishment and finally force their way into her den, she provided still another safeguard.

THE SECRET OF THE CHIMNEY

"Mother" Mandelbaum had a special chimney built in her den, where she kept a little wood fire burning during the winter and kept the fireplace filled with old trash during the hot season. This chimney was peculiarly constructed, and had a false back behind the fire, and in this cavity was hidden a little dumb-waiter. In front of the dumb-waiter was a false iron chimney back on a hinge that could be let down. She constructed a special brick wall so that it appeared to be the regular wall of the house.

In case of sudden emergency, "Mother" Mandelbaum could gather up any diamonds or stolen goods which might be incriminating, pull down the false chimney back, which fell down over the fire, stow away the telltale valuable in the hidden dumb-waiter, push the dumb-waiter up out of sight into the chimney, and push back into place the false chimney back. This simple operation concluded, "Mother" Mandelbaum was then ready to face a search or a holdup.

Gradually "Mother" Mandelbaum's clientele of crooks increased in number and importance until she had only one real rival, John D. Grady, known as "Old Supers and Slangs."

Grady had a more distinguished body of bank burglars under his sway than had "Mother." Bank burglars are the aristocrats of the underworld, just as pickpockets are the lowest.

When the Manhattan Bank robbery was planned and executed, "Mother" Mandelbaum was much humiliated that she could not command the financing and planning of the splendid project. It was Grady's funds which financed the undertaking, and poor "Mother" lost her one pet and star, "Western George" Howard. Howard, in many ways, was the greatest of bank burglars, and he was rated by many as superior to Grady's Jimmy Hope. In another chapter I told you how "Western George" made the Manhattan Bank robbery possible and then was murdered.

After Grady's tragic death, "Mother" Mandelbaum was the undisputed financier, guide, counselor, and friend of crime in New York.

For twenty-five years she lived on the proceeds of other people's crimes. During that time she made many millions. But these millions slipped away for the most part in bribing, fixing, and silencing people.

Still she was a very wealthy, fat, ugly old woman when the blow fell. Mary Holbrook, a shoplifter and old-time ally of Mrs. Mandelbaum, had a serious row with her. This row was the beginning of "Mother's" end.

Soon after Mary was arrested, and, of course, applied for help from the usual source. Not a cent would the old woman give her for bail, counsel fees, or even for special meals in the Tombs. Mary was desperate, and sent for the District Attorney. It just happened that District Attorney Olney was an honest man. He listened to Mary's tale about "Mother" Mandelbaum, and acted.

"Mother" Mandelbaum, her son Julius, and Herman Stoude, one of her employees, were arrested.

"Abe" Hummel did his best, but the indictment held, and there was a mass of evidence sure to swamp her at the trial. But "Mother" did not wait for the trial. She and the others "jumped" their bail and escaped to Canada.

Here she lived a few years a wretched and broken figure, yearning and working to get back to the haunts she loved. But neither her money nor her political friends were able to secure her immunity.

Once she did sneak to New York for a few hours and escaped unnoticed. It was at the time of her daughter's funeral, which she watched from a distance, unable to attend publicly.

Though "Mother" Mandelbaum had money when she died, yet she was an exiled, broken-hearted old woman, whose money did her no good. Unusually talented woman that she was, it took most of her lifetime for her to learn the lesson that crime does not pay!

And now let us take a look at Grady, Mrs. Mandelbaum's great rival. Did this remarkable man find that crime paid in the long run?

GRADY THE DARING

John D. Grady, known to the police and the underworld as "Old Supers and Slangs," probably never handled as much money or had his finger in quite so many crimes as "Mother" Mandelbaum. His career, too, was somewhat shorter, but it made up for these defects in the unequaled daring and magnitude of his exploits.

"Mother" Mandelbaum "played safe." Not so John D. Grady. His was a desperate game, well played for splendid stakes, with risks few men would care to take, and with all the elements of romance and a tragic death to cap it.

Grady, like "Mother" Mandelbaum, was a "fence," but, while she dealt in everything, Grady specialized in diamonds. He had an office opposite the Manhattan Bank that bore the sign "John D. Grady, Diamond Merchant." From the windows of this office, Grady, Jimmy Hope, and his gang gazed hungrily across at the bank and plotted its ruin. Up to the actual day of the robbery, Hope and Grady were in accord on all plans. Afterward the two leaders quarreled over the disposition of the bonds. Hope had his way and there is little doubt that had Grady taken charge of the two million dollars of securities he would have succeeded in selling them, whereas Hope failed.

While "Mother" Mandelbaum was building up her trade with pickpockets and shoplifters, Grady was carrying his business about in a satchel. No man ever took greater chances. At all hours of the night this short, stocky man went about the darkest and most dangerous parts of New York. In the little black satchel, as every criminal knew, was a fortune in diamonds.

When a thief had made a haul, Grady would meet him at any time or place he pleased and take the diamonds off his hands. Only once was he "sandbagged" and robbed of several thousand dollars worth of the stones. He took the misfortune in good part, said it was his own fault, and never took revenge on the men who robbed him.

STEAM-DRILL BURGLARY

While "Mother" Mandelbaum engineered house and dry goods store robberies, Grady set his mind and energies on the great banks. As bold as the Manhattan affair was his assault on a West Side bank. The vaults of this bank were surrounded by a three-foot wall of solid concrete.

Grady opened a first-class saloon next door, and as soon as he got his bearings installed a steam engine in the cellar. This engine was supposed to run the electric light dynamo and an air pump. In reality it was there to drill a hole into the bank next door.

Selecting a Saturday which happened to be a holiday, he commenced operations Friday night, and there was every prospect of being inside the vault long before Monday morning. But, unfortunately, a wide-awake policeman of inquiring mind heard the unfamiliar buzzing out in the street. He prowled around and finally discovered that something unusual was going on in the cellar under the saloon. No answer coming to his knocks, he burst in the door and descended to the cellar. The thieves ran out, but two were caught in the street. Though Grady financed and planned this scheme, he escaped untouched, for there was no evidence against him.

Criminals, successful and unsuccessful, rarely lack women to love them. Strangely enough, this grim, daring, successful general of crime was perpetually spurned and flouted by my sex. Finally there came to him like an angel from heaven a very beautiful, well-bred daughter of the rich. Of course, John fell in love with her—any man would have—and things looked favorable for him.

This woman was the young and almost penniless widow of a member of the "four hundred." She had involved herself in a financial situation from which there was no honest escape. Just as servants of the rich ran to "Mother" Mandelbaum with their secrets, so this woman went to Grady with her inside knowledge.

A sort of partnership sprang up between them which was profitable to both, but particularly to the woman, who used her sex unhesitatingly to get the better of her bargains with the cunning old master of the underworld. Grady's passion grew stronger and stronger, and the young widow, who really despised him, found it harder and harder to keep him at a distance.

Finally things came to a head. Grady knew that the secret of the Manhattan Bank was soon to come out and that his position in New York would be no longer safe. He was ready to flee, but his passion for the woman had become so completely his master that he would not move without her. It was a peculiar duel of wits that followed. The woman was financially dependent on Grady and dared not hide from him nor pretend that she did not return his passion.

The night came when she must either elope with him or lose his aid. The thought of either was unbearable, yet she met him in his empty house at midnight prepared. She knew that Grady would have his entire fortune with him in the form of the diamonds and her plan was nothing less than to murder him and take his jewels. She had brought a little vial of poison with her and held it in trembling fingers within her muff. She knew Grady had a bottle of yellow wine, and she knew it would not be hard to have him drink a toast to their elopement.

Grady produced the bottle but also only one dirty tumbler. They were both to drink from that, it seemed. The woman, at her wits' ends, glanced about the room and spied a battered tin cup.

"There," she cried, pointing, "the very thing."

GRADY'S ROMANTIC DEATH

While Grady went to get it she emptied the vial into the dirty glass. Grady soon poured a quantity of the yellow wine on top of it, and then filled the cup. But to her horror, he handed her the glass and took the cup.

"No, no, John," she gasped, "you take the glass. I'll drink from the cup."

"Why," asked Grady, his eyes aflame with sudden suspicion, "what's the matter?"

"Oh, only that I left a kiss for you on the glass," she faltered.

Grady took the glass and slowly, very slowly, he raised it toward his lips, all the while gazing unwinkingly at the woman. Just at his lips the glass stopped and the woman could not avoid a shudder, she covered her eyes and Grady, used to reading people's minds, read hers. He let the glass fall and shouted:

"So, it's murder you want—well, murder it shall be, but I'll do the murdering."

She saw death in his eyes as he seized her arm but before death he would first have his way with her. She screamed and, pulling with the strength of despair, twisted the arm out of Grady's grasp, leaving half her sleeve in his hand.

Still, there could surely be no hope for her, and yet at that very instant when he poised himself to plunge after her again, his eyes turned glassy; paralysis seized him, and he sank slowly into his chair while the fainting woman tottered out of the door.

The next day, it so happened, Shevelin, the watchman, confessed to his connection with the Manhattan Bank robbery. The police were just taking up the trail that led to Grady's connection with the affair when the news came to headquarters that Grady was dead.

He was found with the sleeve of a woman's dress grasped convulsively in his hand. On the table were a bottle of wine and a cup. A broken glass and spilled wine on the floor showed traces of poison.

CREED OF THE "FENCES"

An autopsy performed on Grady's body showed no sign of poison. His death had been caused by apoplexy. The woman who meant to kill him by poison had actually done so by means of the furious emotions she had aroused. She could have taken the diamonds had she only dared to wait.

Thus died Grady, still free from the law, and with his great fortune in diamonds in his pocket. Yet he died in an agony of furious disappointment as miserably as it is the lot of man to die. For him, as for "Mother" Mandelbaum, it was destined that the lesson should be finally but tragically impressed—that crime does not pay!

As a general thing the receiver of stolen goods is the greediest, tightest-fisted individual who ever squeezed a dollar. The bargains he drives are so one-sided that unless the thief is unusually shrewd he will find his profits dwindling to almost nothing by the time he has disposed of his plunder. The margin between what the thief gets for his stealings and the price they finally bring is enormous, and even with only a few thieves working regularly for him the "fence" finds it easy to get rich in a very short time.

The greed of the "fences" is one important reason why many criminals find it difficult to reform. The more thieves a "fence" has working for him the greater his profits, and naturally the longer they remain in the business the more valuable they are. When a thief reforms, the "fence" is put to the trouble and expense of training a new man—and there is always the danger that the new member of the staff will prove less capable or industrious than the one whose place he takes.

The "fence," therefore, tries to make crime so attractive or so necessary to the clever thief that he will continue stealing until death or arrest overtakes him. He keeps close watch for signs of a desire to reform, and does all he can to discourage it.

The "fence" studies the special weaknesses of his thieves and understands just how to play on them to his advantage. If a thief suggests "turning over a new leaf," the "fence" pays him more liberally for his next lot of goods, or loans him money to satisfy his craving for liquor, drugs, fine clothes, or whatever may be his failing.

This last is a favorite method of getting a thief into a "fence's" power. The "fence" advances money freely, with the "always-glad-to-help-an-old-friend" spirit. But he keeps careful count of every dollar loaned, and when the inevitable day of reckoning comes the debt is usually so large that the thief can never hope to pay it except by crime.

SHINBURN AND THE FENCE

After living an honest life for fifteen years, Mark Shinburn might never have turned burglar again had he not fallen into the hands of one of these avaricious receivers of stolen goods.

Shinburn—as I will tell you in a later chapter—had accumulated from his early robberies a million dollars. With this fortune he went to Belgium, bought an estate and the title of count, and settled down to the life of a prosperous country gentleman.

But the evil fortune which seems to follow every thief never forsook Shinburn. His mania for gambling and an unlucky series of speculations in the stock market at last left him penniless.

In the hope of restoring his fallen fortunes, Shinburn went to London. There he met an old acquaintance of his—a wealthy receiver of stolen goods. This wily trickster, eager to get Shinburn, the greatest of burglars, to stealing for him again, received him with open arms,

"Glad to accommodate you, Mark," said the "fence" when a loan was suggested. "Your word is good for whatever you need—and pay it back whenever you are able."

The money Shinburn received in this way went where much of his original fortune had gone—at Monte Carlo. He returned to the London "fence" for another loan, and another—and all were willingly granted. But when he sought money the fourth time he found the "fence's" attitude strangely changed.

HE TURNS BURGLAR AGAIN

"Really," said the "fence," "I don't see how I can let you have any more money. It seems peculiar that you should be in such straitened circumstances. In the old days you used to have all the money you needed— why don't you use your wits and get some now?"

After touching Shinburn's pride in this crafty way, the "fence" casually mentioned an excellent opportunity which had come to his ears for robbing a bank in Belgium. It was, he said, a rather delicate undertaking, but there was a great deal of money involved—and Shinburn was the one man in the world who could carry it through.

Shinburn's shame at being obliged to borrow money made him an easy victim of the "fence's" wiles. He went to Belgium, was caught in the act of entering the bank, and was sent to prison for a long term. As soon as he was released the London "fence" began pressing him for money, and Shinburn became a confirmed criminal again, primarily to pay this debt.

And this same "fence," Einstein by name, paid the penalty of his wretched practices with a bullet in his brain, which was sent there by a desperate burglar who had tried vainly to reform but was held in criminal bondage by Einstein.

The promoter of crime is not always a receiver of stolen goods. Sometimes he is himself a thief, who has mastered some branch of the business so thoroughly that he is able to sit back and let others do the active work.

Such a man was "Dutch Dan" Watson, who was long considered one of the most expert makers of duplicate keys in America. His specialty was entering buildings and taking wax impressions of the keys, which he often found hanging up in surprisingly convenient places.

From these impressions Watson, in his own workshop, would make the duplicate keys and file them away for future use. To each key he would attach a tag bearing the address of the building and a little diagram showing the exact location of the door which the key unlocked.

"Dutch Dan's" active part in the proposed crime ended as soon as the keys were made. Then, from the wide circle of criminals that he knew, he would select a number of expert burglars and hand them a set of the keys and diagrams, showing just how the robbery was to be carried out.

If the burglars were successful they turned over to "Dutch Dan" 20 per cent, of the proceeds. This mode of operation proved very profitable for Watson, and I remember that he often had as many as eight different parties of burglars working for him at one time.

And Watson, like Einstein, was sent to his grave by a fellow criminal, who had been discarded from his gang and killed him in revenge.

Will any reader who has reviewed with me the lives of the famous criminals recounted above dispute my assertion that, truly, crime does not pay?

CHAPTER IX

SURPRISING METHODS OF THE THIEVES WHO WORK ONLY DURING BUSINESS HOURS AND WALK AWAY WITH THOUSANDS OF DOLLARS UNDER THE VERY EYES OF THE BANK OFFICIALS

ONE DAY BEFORE I WAS AS WELL KNOWN TO THE POLICE AS I LATER became I was walking down Broadway in New York when I met a prominent citizen of the underworld with whom I had been associated in numerous burglaries. So far as I knew at that time he was still a burglar. After we had stood chatting for several minutes I was surprised to have him press a hundred-dollar bill into my hand and say:

"Just as the clocks strike noon today I want you to go into the Manhattan Bank and have this bill changed. Walk right up to the paying teller's window and ask for some silver and small bills. When he hands you the money take your time about counting it, and keep his attention engaged just as long as you can."

"But what do I get for running errands for you?" I jokingly inquired.

He refused to explain any further, and, as I was just dying with curiosity to find out what sort of game he was up to, I agreed to do as I was told. Of course, I knew it was some crime he was inveigling me into, but just what it was, or what part I was playing in it, I had no more idea than a babe unborn when I strolled into the bank promptly on the stroke of twelve.

The paying teller proved to be a very susceptible man, and I found no difficulty in getting him into conversation. As there were few people in the bank at that hour, he was glad enough to relieve the monotony of his day's work by a little chat with a pretty young woman.

Well, to make a long story short, we talked busily for fully fifteen minutes, and during all that time I succeeded in keeping his eyes riveted on me. When, at last, a man approached the window to transact some business I put my money away in my satchel, gave the courteous teller a parting smile, and strolled leisurely out of the bank. While I was in the bank I had seen nothing of the man who had sent me on this mysterious errand, and I did not see him until I called at his hotel that evening.

"We've done a good day's work, Sophie, and here is your share of the profits," he said, handing me a fatter roll of crisp bank notes than I had laid my hands on for several weeks. As I hurriedly counted the bills over I was amazed to find that the roll contained $2,000.

"While you were flirting so deliciously with the paying teller," my friend explained," I slipped into the bank by a side entrance, reached my hand through a gate in the wire cage and grabbed a bundle of bills, which I later found to contain $4,000."

That was my introduction to the work of the "bank sneak"—a thief whose methods were then in their infancy, but who developed ingenuity and boldness so rapidly that he soon became the terror of the banks and every business man who ever has to handle large sums of money or securities.

What I have to tell you today about "bank sneaks" and their methods will furnish as good an example as anything I know of the fact that crime does not pay.

The stealings of a clever "sneak" often run as high as $100,000 in a single year. But what benefit does he get out of this easily acquired wealth? It invariably goes as easily as it comes, and, after a few months, he is as badly in need of money as he was before. I can count on the fingers of one hand the "sneaks" who are getting any real happiness out of life—and they are all men and women who, like myself, have seen the error of their ways and reformed.

If crime could ever prove profitable to any man, it would have proved so to Walter Sheridan, long the foremost "bank sneak" in America. So varied and far reaching were his adroit schemes that within twenty years the gangs which he organized and led stole more than a million dollars. He was a past master in the art of escaping punishment for his crimes, and he was also a shrewd, close-fisted financier, who claimed the lion's share of all the booty and carefully hoarded his savings.

Yet what did all his cleverness avail this prince of "sneaks?" His fortune was swept away, and he finally died a pauper in the prison cell to which he was sent when he was picked up starving in the streets of Montreal.

Sheridan introduced many ingenious new methods in "bank sneaking," just as Mark Shinburn did in burglary. He was the first to conceal a pair of tweezers in the end of his cane and use them to pick up bundles of money which were beyond the reach of his arms.

This cane was a really wonderful device. To all appearances it was only a fine, straight piece of bamboo, nicely polished and fitted with an ivory handle—the sort of walking stick any prosperous man might carry.

Only when you unscrewed its heavy brass ferrule was the dishonest purpose for which it was intended revealed. The bamboo stick was hollow, and in it were two narrow strips of steel which dropped down below the end of the cane and could be operated like tweezers when you released the spring, which was concealed under a heavy band of solid silver just below the handle.

When Sheridan was his natural self he was a stout, good looking man of dignified presence and refined manners who would readily pass for a well-to-do merchant or manufacturer. But when occasion required he could change his appearance so that even his closest friends wouldn't recognize him.

Once when he was arrested in New York he effected in his cell in the Tombs a transformation which mystified the authorities and nearly resulted in his release on the ground of mistaken identity.

He exchanged his expensively tailored suit and fine linen for the dirty rags of a tramp who was locked up in the adjoining cell. With a broken knife blade he hacked off every bit of his long flowing beard. He dyed his reddish brown hair with coffee grounds and clipped and twisted it to make it look a life-long stranger to comb and brush. By eating soap he managed to reduce his portly figure to a thin, sickly shadow of skin and bones.

When the prison keepers came to take him into court for trial they were amazed to find in place of the well-dressed, well-fed broker they had locked up a few days before a repulsively dirty, ragged, emaciated tramp, whose actions indicated that he was not more than half witted.

This ruse of Sheridan's failed, however, through the persistence of William A. Pinkerton, head of the Pinkerton Detective Agency. Mr. Pinkerton, who had been on Sheridan's trail for years, identified him positively in spite of his changed appearance, and succeeded in having him convicted and sentenced to five years in Sing Sing prison.

It was from this wizard of crime, Walter Sheridan, that I learned the value of the clever disguises which so often stood me in good stead and which enabled my comrades and me to get our hands on hundreds of thousands of dollars that didn't belong to us.

Early in my career I conceived the idea of furthering my dishonest plans by posing as a wealthy old widow, so crippled that she had to transact whatever business she had with the bank from her seat in her carriage. This plan succeeded beyond my fondest expectations, and I am ashamed to think how many thousands of dollars I stole through this simple but extremely effective little expedient.

This ruse proved its merits the first time we tried it—in the daylight robbery of a Brooklyn, New York bank, where one of my two companions walked away with $40,000 while I sat outside in my carriage listening to the old cashier's advice about investing the money my lamented husband had left me.

But let me go back to the very beginning and show you just how this bold robbery was planned and carried out.

We had had our eyes on this bank for a week—Johnny Meaney, Tom Bigelow, and I. Between the hours of 12 and 1 each day we found there were few customers in the bank and the institution was left in charge of the old cashier and a young bookkeeper.

But the cashier, although over sixty years old, was a keen-eyed, nervous man, whose suspicions were apt to be easily aroused. And, besides, the window in the wire cage where he did business with the bank's customers was so situated that he could always see out of the corner of his eye the vault and the long counter where the money was piled.

We all agreed that it was not safe to attempt the robbery while the cashier was in his usual place.

If I could only devise some way of getting him outside the bank for a few minutes it would be easy for one of the men to hold the young bookkeeper in conversation at the paying teller's window, which was so placed that while he stood there his back was toward the vault. That would give just the opportunity we needed for the third member of the party to step unnoticed through a convenient side door and get the plunder.

But how to lure the cashier out of the bank? That was the question, and it was while I was racking my brains for some solution of the difficulty that I blundered upon the idea of posing as a wealthy widow who was too lame to leave her carriage when she called at the bank.

During my stay in this city I had heard of the death in Europe of a rich and prominent Brooklyn man. He had been living abroad for the last ten years and had married there an English woman who had never visited Brooklyn and was entirely unknown there except by name.

Nothing could have suited my purpose better. I would pose as this wealthy Brooklyn man's widow, and in this guise would induce the bank cashier to come out to my carriage and talk with me.

You may be sure that I laid my plans with the greatest care, for I knew what a bold undertaking this was and that the least oversight on my part would spoil everything.

First I bought a silver gray wig to cover my chestnut hair. It was a beautiful specimen of the wigmaker's art and cost me sixty-five dollars.

Then I made up my plump, rosy cheeks to look as pale and wrinkled as an invalid woman's should at the age of seventy and dressed myself in the gloomiest, most expensive widow's weeds I could find.

A pair of hideous blue goggles and two crutches completed my disguise. The glasses were to hide my bright eyes, whose habit of roaming incessantly from side to side I had an idea often made people suspicious of me; and the crutches were to bear out my story of the paralyzed limbs which made my leaving my carriage except when absolutely necessary out of the question.

My costume was not the only detail which had to be arranged to make my plan complete. I must have some visiting cards—cards with a heavy mourning border and the name of the Brooklyn man's widow engraved on them.

I also didn't forget to place with these cards in my handbag some worthless mining stock which had been my share of a western bank robbery, and which even Ellen Peck's shrewd magic couldn't turn into cash. This would be useful, I thought, in holding the old cashier's attention.

Then there were my horses and a carriage befitting my wealth which the men hired from a livery stable. I called on two young thieves whom I knew over in New York, and, by promising them a small percentage of whatever we succeeded in stealing, induced them to dress up in some borrowed livery and act as my driver and footman.

At last everything was arranged and the day was set for the robbery. The morning dawned warm and bright—just the sort of weather which would make an invalid widow feel like venturing out to transact a little business.

I had not seen Bigelow and Meaney since the night before. They had called then at my rooms to go over our plans for the last time. Bigelow was to engage the attention of the bookkeeper, who would be left alone in the bank after the cashier's departure, while wiry little Johnny Meaney made his way through the side door and got the money.

At a few minutes past twelve my carriage drew up in front of the bank. Two or three of the officials were just going to lunch. If nothing unexpected had happened to change the bank's routine, the cashier and one bookkeeper were alone in the counting-room and the coast was clear.

Through my blue glasses I could see Tom Bigelow's big form swinging down the street as unconcernedly as if he had not a care in the world. And from the opposite direction, although I could not see him, I felt positive that Meaney was on his way to carry out his part in our crime.

The footman jumped down and stood at attention while I fumbled in my bag for one of my black bordered cards. With hands which trembled naturally enough to give the last touch of reality to my feeble appearance I handed him the card and tremulously

POSING AS A WEALTHY WIDOW

whispered my instructions. He bowed respectfully and disappeared inside the bank.

Would the cashier be good enough to step outside and discuss a little matter of business with a lady who was unable to leave her carriage?

The cashier is very sorry but he is extremely busy and, as he is practically alone in the bank just now, it will be impossible for him to leave his desk. Can't the lady arrange to step inside for a minute?

Before the nervous footman has time to explain that the lady is a cripple and cannot leave her carriage the cashier has taken another look at the card, has recognized the name, and realizes that it is the widow of a millionaire who is waiting outside for an audience with him.

"Oh, I beg your pardon," he says nervously; "the light is so poor here that I could hardly see that name. Tell the lady that I will be out directly." As the footman walks out to report to his mistress that her wishes are going to be fulfilled the cashier hurriedly changes the linen jacket he wears at his desk for a solemn frock coat, gives his scanty hair a quick part and calls to the bookkeeper to look out for things while he is gone.

All this time I am sitting primly there in the carriage trying as hard as I know how to live up to the dignity of a millionaire's widow and to conceal my fears that something is going to happen to disarrange our carefully laid plans.

But, the next instant, I am relieved to see the cashier coming toward me all bows and smiles. And, as he comes out of the bank he almost brushes elbows with Tom Bigelow, who, with a punctuality worthy of a better cause, is going into the bank at that very moment.

Yes, indeed, the cashier remembers my husband and he is proud of the opportunity to be of some service to his widow. I can see the avarice shining in his eyes as he thinks of the profits his bank will make if he can get the handling of my property.

Our interview is, of course, a tedious affair for I am very feeble and have all sorts of difficulty in finding the mining stock about which I want to consult him. But the cashier shows not the slightest impatience and humors my whims with all the consideration my wealth and position deserve.

And, when he sees what a worthless lot of stock I have invested in, his interest in me becomes all the greater.

Out of the corner of my eye I can just see Tom Bigelow as he stands talking with the bookkeeper inside the bank. And, by this time, if no unforeseen difficulty has arisen, I know that Johnny Meaney is in the vault making a quick but judicious selection of the cash and securities which we can most easily dispose of.

After what seemed an eternity, but was in reality only four or five minutes, I saw Bigelow come out of the bank and stroll leisurely up the street. This was the signal that the money had been secured and that Meaney was making his escape in the opposite direction.

Now everything depended on my holding the cashier just as much longer as I could. Every minute he remained there talking with me meant that much delay in the discovery of the bank's loss and the starting of the police on our trail.

Another five minutes dragged along before I had exhausted the supply of questions which I wanted answered. Then I said goodbye, promising to return on the next day, and told my coachman to drive on. The cashier whom I had duped so successfully stood there on the sidewalk bowing and smiling as my carriage rolled down the street.

I went to the house of a friend, where I exchanged my disguise for my ordinary clothes. Then I boarded a train for Montreal and there a few days later Bigelow and Meaney divided with me booty amounting to $40,000.

It was nothing unusual for the clever bands of "bank sneaks" with which I "worked" to steal as much or more than that in as short order. But, as I have told you, a relentless curse followed our dishonestly acquired wealth and, sooner or later, taught those who would learn the lesson that honesty is the only policy and that crime does not pay.

CHAPTER X

STARTLING SURPRISES THAT CONFRONT CRIMINALS—HOW UNEXPECTED HAPPENINGS SUDDENLY DEVELOP AND UPSET CAREFULLY LAID PLANS AND CAUSE THE BURGLARS ARREST OR PREVENT HIS GETTING EXPECTED PLUNDER

ONLY ONE WHO HAS BEEN, AS I HAVE, FOR YEARS BEHIND THE SCENES at all sorts of crimes can appreciate how often every criminal is brought face to face with the most startling surprises.

No matter how clever a robber is he can never tell when arrest, serious injury, or death will bring his dishonest career to a sudden end. And, even if he escapes these fatal disasters, there are always a thousand and one chances which may develop at any moment to spoil his carefully laid plans and prevent his getting his plunder. Most of these are things which it is absolutely impossible to foresee and guard against. This is why only a small percentage of the crimes which are attempted ever succeed and why their success hangs trembling in the balance until the very last minute.

The brains we criminals expended in saving some robbery from failure or in escaping the consequences of our deeds would have won us lasting success and happiness in any honorable pursuit—used, as they were, for crime, they brought us in the end only disgrace and remorse. That is the lesson which these experiences have taught me and which I hope every reader of this page will learn.

If there was ever a thief who planned his crimes with greater attention to the smallest details than Harry Raymond, the man who stole the famous Gainsborough, I never knew him.

But even Raymond's painstaking care was not proof against all the startling surprises which confronted him and his plans were often completely ruined by one of these unexpected happenings.

Raymond was always a restless man—never content to remain long in one place. When stories of the rich gold and diamond mines in South Africa reached his ears he began to cast longing eyes in that direction. Where there was so much treasure, he thought, there surely ought to be an opportunity to get his hands on a share of it.

He tried to induce Mark Shinburn to go with him, but Shinburn had his eye on several big robberies nearer home, and so Raymond set out alone. On the way he met Charley King, a noted English thief, and the two joined forces.

Raymond hadn't been in South Africa twenty-four hours before he learned that a steamer left Cape Town for England every week with a heavy shipment of gold and diamonds on board. His next step was to find out just how this treasure was brought down from the mines.

As he soon learned, it came by stage each week, the day before the steamer sailed. The bags of gold dust and uncut diamonds were locked in a strongbox which was carried under the driver's seat. There was only one other man on the coach besides the driver—a big, powerful Boer, who carried a brace of revolvers and a repeating rifle and had the reputation of being a dead shot.

There was just one difficulty in the way—Raymond really needed a third man to assist King and him. Among all the criminals in Cape

Town whom he knew there was none he could trust, and so he at last decided to ask a wholly inexperienced man to join the party. The man he selected was an American sea captain who had been obliged to flee from his native land after setting fire to his ship for the insurance. He was desperately in need of money and was, therefore, only too glad of the opportunity to share in the fortune Raymond proposed to steal.

Raymond, with his customary caution, studied the proposition from every angle. At last he was convinced that he had provided for every contingency which could possibly arise to prevent his robbery of the coach.

This was his plan—to stretch a rope across some lonely spot in the road and trip the horses. Before the driver and the guard could recover from their astonishment and extricate themselves from the overturned coach, Raymond and his companions would leap from their ambush and overpower them.

Half way up a long hill, down which the coach would come, the three men concealed themselves—Raymond and the captain on one side of the road, King on the other.

Around a tree on either side of the road they fastened the rope with a slip noose, letting its length lie loose on the ground directly in the path of the coach. Carefully loading their revolvers they settled down to wait for its approach.

At last their ears caught the rumble of its wheels and presently the four horses which drew the heavy vehicle and its precious contents appeared above the crest of the hill. They were making good time on the last lap of their long journey from the mines.

On they came, until the hoofs of the leaders were within a foot of the rope. Raymond gave a shrill whistle and his companions stretched the rope tight across the road at a distance of about two feet above the ground.

As the forward horses struck the barrier they fell in a heap and the ones behind came tumbling on top of them. The wagon pole snapped like a pipe stem.

The heavy coach stopped short, reeled uncertainly for a second, then keeled over on its side, hurling both the driver and the guard several feet away.

The three robbers sprang from their hiding place and covered the prostrate men with their revolvers.

As they did so one of the fallen horses scrambled to his feet, broke the remnants of the harness that clung to him and dashed down the hill, furious with pain and fear.

Not one of the robbers paid any heed to this incident—for who would have suspected that a frightened stage horse could interfere with their carefully-laid plans?

The driver was easily disposed of, but the guard showed fight and it required the combined efforts of the three men to bind and gag him so that he could do no harm.

They were just knotting a piece of rope around his struggling legs when a shot rang out and a rifle bullet whizzed by their heads—followed by another and another.

An instant before the moon had broken through the clouds. By its light they saw six sturdy Boer farmers advancing up the hill, firing their repeating rifles as they came.

Resistance was useless—they were outnumbered two to one and they had all been in South Africa long enough to have a wholesome respect for a Boer's marksmanship.

Covering their retreat with a few shots from their revolvers, they took to their heels. In the rain of bullets which was falling around them it was suicide to think of trying to take the heavy strong box with them, and they had to leave it there in the coach with all its treasure untouched.

Raymond was completely mystified. He and his companions had not fired a shot in their struggle with the men on the coach. How had those Boer farmers, who lived in a house at the foot of the hill nearly half a mile away, happened to be aroused just in time to spoil the robbery?

The account the newspapers gave of the robbery cleared up the mystery. It seemed that the frightened horse which had dashed down the hill had plunged through the lattice gate in the front of the Boer's house.

The crash of the woodwork and the wounded animal's cries of pain as he struggled to free himself had awakened the farmers. As they rushed out half dressed to see what the trouble was the moon shone out and revealed to them the overturned coach on the hillside above and the robbers struggling with the guard and driver.

You see what a surprising thing it all was and how impossible it was for Raymond to have foreseen that anything like this would happen. But these two little incidents—the runaway horse and the moon's sudden appearance—were all that was needed to snatch away $250,000 in gold and diamonds just as Raymond thought he had it safely in his hands.

Even more surprising was what happened when Tom Smith and I, with Dan Nugent and George Mason, were trying to rob a little bank down in Virginia.

The fact that the cashier and his family lived on the floor above this bank made it a rather ticklish undertaking.

There was, however, no vault to enter, and the safe was such a ramshackle affair that the men felt sure they could open it without the use of a charge of powder. So we decided to make the attempt.

As Tom Smith had sprained his wrist in escaping from a Pennsylvania sheriff a few nights before he was to remain on guard outside the bank, while I entered with Dan and George and rendered what assistance I could in opening the safe. This was the first time I had ever been on the "inside" of a bank burglary and I was quite puffed up with my own importance.

Dan opened one of the bank windows with his jimmy and held his hands for me to step on as I drew myself up over the high sill. Then he handed the tools to me and he and George climbed up.

The bank in which we found ourselves was one large room. A door led into it from the broad porch which extended along the front of the building. At the rear was another door opening into a long passageway, at the end of which was a staircase leading to the cashier's apartments overhead.

While the two men were looking the safe over I unlocked the front door to provide an avenue of escape in case we should have to beat a hasty retreat.

I also opened the door at the rear and peered into the darkness of the passageway. There was no sign of life—no sound except the heavy breathing of the sleeping cashier and his family in the rooms above. I closed the door gently for fear the rasping of the drills on the metal of the safe would be heard.

Just then my quick ears caught the sound of someone in the passageway. I tiptoed over to the door and pressed my ear against it.

I had barely time to draw away from the door before it opened wide and I stood speechless with amazement at the apparition I saw standing there within an arm's length of me.

I am not a superstitious woman, but what I saw in that doorway set my heart to thumping madly, and sent the cold shivers up and down my back. And I am not ashamed to confess how startled I was, for Dan Nugent and George Mason, the veterans of a hundred burglaries, later admitted that nothing had ever given them such a scare as this.

What we saw facing us, like a ghost, was a beautiful young woman. The filmy white night robe she wore left her snowy arms and shoulders bare and revealed her bare feet.

Her face looked pale and ghastly in the light of the kerosene lamp she carried high in one hand. The mass of jet black hair which crowned her head and hung in a long braid down her back made her pallor all the more death-like.

Her eyes were shut tight.

For a minute we stood blinking like frightened children at this uncanny, white, silent figure. Then, gradually, it dawned on us that this apparition was the cashier's eldest daughter, and that she was walking in her sleep.

As we recovered our senses it didn't take us long to see what a dangerous situation we were in. At any moment our unwelcome visitor might awaken. By the time we could bind and gag her the rest of the family might discover her absence and start in search of her.

The girl looked so innocent and helpless and so strangely beautiful that, for my part, I was heartily glad when George Mason nodded his head toward the door to indicate that we would better be going.

The two men climbed out of the window and I made my escape by the front door. The last I saw of the sleep-walking girl she was

SURPRISED BY A SLEEP WALKER

groping her way across the bank with slow cautious steps, still holding the lamp high above her head and looking more than ever like a graveyard specter.

Whether anybody except ourselves ever knew what a strange chance saved the bank from robbery that night I never heard. It was a costly experience for us as, according to what we learned later from the newspapers, that safe contained $20,000 in cash.

We missed that tidy little bit of plunder just because a young woman was addicted to the habit of walking in her sleep.

And now another instance—the very remarkable chain of surprises which resulted in the murder of a bank cashier, the blackening of a dead man's reputation, and, finally, the imprisonment of two desperate burglars for life.

For many years the robbery of the bank in Dexter, Maine, puzzled everybody. This was a job of national importance, because Mr. Barron, the cashier of the bank, was accidentally murdered, and the detectives, after failing to get any clue to the burglars, buncoed the bank officials by inventing the theory that the unfortunate cashier had murdered himself!

They managed to fix up the books of the bank in such a way as to show some trivial pretended defalcation, which amounted, as I remember it, to about $1,100. On the strength of this barefaced frame-up the memory of the poor cashier was defamed and the bank actually brought suit against the widow for some small sum.

The real facts I will now tell you. Jimmy Hope, the famous bank burglar, first got his eye on the Dexter bank as a promising prospect, and made all his plans to enter the bank when, to his disgust, he was grabbed for another matter and given a prison term. In Jimmy Hope's gang was an ambitious burglar named David L. Stain, and Stain decided that there was no reason why the Dexter bank should escape simply because Hope was serving a sentence.

So Stain looked over the ground and decided to rob the bank with a little band of his own, consisting of Oliver Cromwell and a man named Harvey, and somebody else whose name I do not now recall. They selected Washington's Birthday because it was a holiday, and there was every reason to believe that nobody would be in the bank.

Late in the afternoon Stain and his associates forced their way into the building and sprung the lock of the back door of the bank. The burglars stood for a moment to put on their masks and rubber shoes, and then Stain moved forward toward the inner room of the bank, where the bank vaults were.

Just at the moment that Stain put his hand on the doorknob Cashier Barron on the other side of the door put his own hand on the inside knob as he unsuspectingly started to leave the inside room, where he had been going over some of the books that were in the vaults.

As the door opened Dave Stain and Cashier Barron suddenly came face to face without the slightest warning. Barron stood paralyzed

AS THE DOOR OPENED STAIN AND BARRON
CAME FACE TO FACE

with astonishment as he peered into the masked face of the leader. Stain, with perfect composure, struck Barron a quick blow with a slung-shot, landing the weapon exactly in the center of Mr. Barron's forehead.

The cashier dropped to the floor stunned and Stain imagined that his victim's skull was crushed, or that, if the blow had not been fatal, Barron would come to his senses and make an outcry. In either case the burglars realized that they had done a bad job. Murder was not intended, and none of the gang had any stomach for going on with the robbery, even though the doors of the big vault stood invitingly open.

After a few moments' hasty consultation the cracksmen picked up the unconscious but still breathing form of the faithful cashier and laid it in the vault, and closed and locked the big doors. Stain and his gang made their way noiselessly out of the building, strolling, one by one, through the town and out into the country, where a span of horses was waiting for them. They drove across country, keeping away from the railroad, and made their escape without leaving a clue of any kind.

When Cashier Barron failed to turn up at home at supper time a search was made and somebody went to the bank. The cashier's hat and coat were found in the inner room, and a faint sound of heavy breathing could be heard from the interior of the closed vault. Blacksmiths were hastily called, and, after several hours' work, succeeded in freeing the imprisoned cashier—but, although Barron was still alive and breathing, his face was black from his having breathed over and over again the poisoned air of the vault, and he died without recovering consciousness.

Several years later a clue to the real truth of the tragedy was picked up by a newspaper reporter, who devoted several weeks of painstaking work to piecing together the scraps of evidence he was able to collect. This reporter then had himself appointed a Massachusetts State detective and arrested Stain and Cromwell, brought them to Bangor, Maine, was able to have them identified by several townspeople who had seen them in Dexter on the day of the murder, and Stain and Cromwell were both convicted of murder in the first degree, and the conviction was unanimously confirmed by the Supreme Court of the State of Maine. They were sentenced to life imprisonment.

I could go on indefinitely recounting instances as surprising as any of these of the unexpected things which are constantly happening to prevent criminals succeeding in their undertakings. But these which I have mentioned are enough to show any thoughtful man or woman how hazardous and how profitless crime always is.

Success in crime is achieved only at the risk of life and liberty. In a few rare cases the criminal escapes these penalties, but, even so, his ill-gotten gains melt rapidly away and bring him no lasting happiness. And, as I have shown here today, a large percentage of the crimes he undertakes yield him nothing for all the time, thought, and effort he has to give them.

Each chapter of my own life, as I am now recalling it, and the lives of all the criminals I have ever known, only give added emphasis to the fact which I want to impress on you— that crime does not pay.

CHAPTER XI

THRILLING EVENTS WHICH CROWDED ONE SHORT WEEK OF MY LIFE HOW I PROFITED NOTHING FROM ALL THE RISKS I FACED

NOT ALL THE CRIMES THE PROFESSIONAL CRIMINAL COMMITS ARE carefully planned in advance. Very often they are committed on the spur of the moment, when the opportunity to steal some article of value without detection suddenly presents itself. The habit of wrong-doing becomes so strongly developed that the thief is unable to resist the temptation to steal even when he is not in need of money and when there is every incentive for him to avoid the risk of arrest.

This was exactly what happened to me in Springfield, Mass., one day. The fact that I was unable to withstand the glittering lure of a tray full of diamonds proved the starting point of one of the most eventful weeks of my life.

What happened to me during the week which began with my bold robbery of a Springfield diamond merchant is as good an example as I can select from my past career to give point to the lesson I have learned and am trying to teach—that crime in the long run can never be made to pay.

Just think of it—in the seven days that followed the unlucky moment when I thrust my hand into that open showcase in Springfield I was arrested three times, jumped my bail once, and successfully made my escape from a Boston cell. During all that time I was never free from fear of arrest—asleep or awake, I would start at the slightest sound, fearful that it was a detective coming to snap those hateful handcuffs on my wrists again.

And what did I have to show for all the nervous strain, all the suffering and hardship I underwent during that week? Worse than nothing at all. Although I stole cash and valuables amounting to more than seven thousand dollars, I was penniless when I finally succeeded in getting back to New York.

A good share of the money had gone to the lawyers. A thousand dollars of it I had been obliged to leave behind when I made my escape from the Boston police, and the trayful of diamond rings I had stolen was hidden in Springfield, where I would not dare show my face for many months. Even the rings on my own fingers had gone to pay my lawyers' fees and my bail.

But let me go back to the very beginning and explain just how all these things came about.

It was when I was on my way back from an unsuccessful bank robbing expedition to a Canadian town. I was feeling tired, out of sorts and generally disgusted with myself. "If I ever get back to my home in New York," I said to myself remorsefully, "I will surely settle down to an honest life."

But alas for all my good intentions! Just before I reached Springfield I happened to recall that this was where an old school friend of mine lived. She was a thoroughly respectable woman, the wife of a hard working tradesman, and I determined to stop off and surprise her with a visit.

As luck would have it, I found her house locked, and one of her neighbors told me that she was away visiting her mother in Worcester. Knowing no one else in Springfield, there was nothing for me to do but kill time for two or three hours until another train left for New York.

I was strolling leisurely along one of the main streets as innocent as one of my babies of any intention of wrongdoing, when I happened to notice something wrong with my watch. The hands had evidently stuck together, and it had stopped more than an hour before. Just across the street I saw a large jewelry store. I walked over there to see about my watch. It was the noon hour and the store was deserted except for an old man whom I judged to be the proprietor, and, at his bench far in the rear, a lone watchmaker.

The proprietor was arranging some trays of diamonds in one of the showcases when I approached him and stated my errand. He said my watch could be fixed in two minutes, and started off with it to the watchmaker's bench. His back was no sooner turned than I took in the fact that he had neglected to close the sliding door of the showcase. Inside there, within easy reach of my long arms, were two, three, a dozen trays of costly diamond rings, brooches, and necklaces.

Forgetting all my recent resolutions and regardless of the consequences I reached my hand across the showcase and down inside. It took a powerful stretch of my muscles to reach the nearest of the trays. But at last my fingers closed securely over its edge, and, with a skill born of long experience, I drew my arm back and the tray of rings came with it.

This was an operation that required a good deal of care, because in my position the tray was not an easy thing to handle without letting some of its precious contents fall clattering to the floor and give the alarm. In less time than it takes to tell, however, and before the proprietor had fairly reached the watchmaker's bench, I had the tray safely concealed in my handbag.

The proprietor returned with my watch. It was only a trivial matter to adjust it, he said, and there would be no charge whatever. I thanked him and hurried out, shaking inwardly for fear he would discover the absence of the tray of rings before I could lose myself in the streets.

After getting his plunder a thief's first thought is to get it out of his possession. What he wants is a temporary hiding place—a place where he can conceal it until whatever outcry the theft may have caused has had time to die down and he can safely dispose of his booty to one of the numerous "fences" who are to be found in every large city. Whenever possible, the prudent thief selects a temporary hiding place before he actually lays his hands on his plunder, and loses no time in getting it out of his possession, so that, in case the police arrest him soon after the robbery, they will find nothing incriminating.

This crime of mine, however, was so entirely unpremeditated that I had not the faintest idea what I was going to do with my tray of rings when I walked out of the store. Down the street a few blocks I saw the railroad station, and this suggested a plan. I would check my bag there and hide the check in some place where I could easily recover it whenever the coast was clear.

This was a plan I had often followed with success, and it is a favorite with thieves even to this day. I saw by the newspapers that the misguided young man who robbed the New York jewelry firm of $100,000 worth of gems the other day went straight to the Pennsylvania Railroad Station and checked the suitcase containing the plunder which had tempted him to his ruin.

By this time all intention of reform had left my mind, and I thought only of the ways I could use the money the diamonds would bring. The hurried inspection I had been able to give them placed their value at fully $3,000.

I walked quickly, but with no outward signs of excitement to the station, where I locked my handbag and exchanged it for a brass check. Then I walked out of the station and seated myself on a bench in the public square. It was the work of only a minute to dig a little cavity in the gravel under one of the legs of the bench with the pointed heel of my French boot. A big red-faced policeman was standing uncomfortably near all the while, but soon he turned his back. I bent over quickly, placed the check in the little hole I had dug, and quickly covered it with earth. I continued sitting there for some minutes, making a mental photograph of the spot so that I would be able to locate it again, even if I had to wait months.

As I rose and crossed the square to a department store I realized that I had not acted a bit too quickly, for I overheard some men discussing the daring robbery of the jewelry store. It had just been discovered, so they said, and the police were already scouring the city for the thieves.

I made haste to purchase a satchel very similar in appearance to the one containing the diamonds. In this I placed a few trinkets and such things as a woman might naturally carry, and returned to the railroad station. I checked this satchel just as I had the other, and walked away—my mind somewhat at rest.

Walking along the main street I encountered a detective who was convoying a couple of men to the station. The face of one of the men was familiar, and he recognized me before I could turn away. Using a store window as a mirror I was able to see that all three had stopped across the street and were looking at me, I lost no time in getting away, and the detective, of course, had his hands full. But I knew my chances of getting out of town were mighty slim, and it was no surprise an hour later when two detectives confronted me at the station.

"How do you do?" said one, "do you live here?"

"I live in New Haven," I said, rapidly adding a fictitious name and address. I explained my visit to town, but they were not satisfied and to the police station I went.

In searching me the detectives held up my satchel check and hurried off gleefully to the depot, quite certain that they had found the missing diamonds.

They returned crestfallen, but the captain had an instinct that told him I had those diamonds and he ordered me locked up overnight.

From a neighboring cell the two men arrested earlier in the day called out: "Hello, Sophie, how did you get in?"

I did not answer, and pretended not to know them. The police unlocked my cell door and invited me to come out and meet my friends, hoping, of course, to learn something.

But I said in a loud voice that I never saw the men before, and that they must have mistaken me. The two men were good enough to take the hint at this point that I was in trouble, and soon after I heard one of them saying that from a distance I looked like Sophie Lyons.

In the morning the police captain reluctantly released me. But he sent a detective to make sure I got out of town, and he gave me his parting promise to run me in if I ever came within his reach.

There was nothing for me to do but to take the train and hope to return some day for the diamonds.

I got off at New Haven and sat in the railroad station pondering ways and means.

My thoughts were interrupted by the appearance of Lizzie Saunders, a woman criminal of no mean ability. From the effusiveness of her welcome I suspected that she was "broke" and wanted a loan, as, indeed, proved to be the case.

I hadn't much to spare, and was forced to listen to her schemes. She told me that the town of Holyoke was a splendid place to pick up money, as it was crowded with farmers attending a fair.

I was tired and disgusted and wanted to return to New York. Yet I did not want to go so far from the diamonds, and, foolishly, I listened and was persuaded.

Arrived at Holyoke we investigated the banks, but saw no chance of snatching anything. We were both very much in need of raising some funds right away, and something had to be done.

A sure-enough farmer cashed a large check, counted the money five times, laid it in a huge wallet, and tied the wallet together with a piece of string. Then he placed it in the breast pocket of his coat and marched out. Of course, we followed. Lizzie, who was known as "The Woman in Black," because she never wore anything else, kept a lookout while I operated.

The old man was watching the street parade, hands in his trousers pockets, chin stuck out, and whiskers projecting a foot in front of him.

I reached my hand into his pocket, got a grip on the wallet, and was about to give the quick snap of the wrist and jostle, which is part of the pickpocket's technique, when I felt a heavy hand on my shoulder. I knew instinctively that it was a detective. Quickly thrusting the bulky wallet back into the old man's pocket, I threw my arms around his neck and kissed him.

I FELT A HAND ON MY SHOULDER

"Oh, Uncle Dan!" I cried between the kisses, with which I fairly smothered the astonished old man, "where in the world did you come from?"

The old man almost got apoplexy, for I kissed him and hugged him with a vehemence that made everybody forget the parade. I can remember the sea of whiskers I dived into.

"Gosh all hemlock, who are you?" he gasped when I let him go. "I ain't Dan, I'm Abijah."

The detective really believed that I knew Abijah, but he remembered Lizzie and took her away. I was about to escape when a redfaced woman arrived and shouted:

"You hussy, what do you mean by hugging my husband?"

The detective hesitated and looked back, but he would have let me go if Lizzy hadn't been fool enough to call out:

"Sophie, find me a lawyer and get me out of this."

That was enough even for the thick-headed police detective, and he took us both away. The old man refused to testify against us. He was afraid he would not be believed and the scandal would have got back to his home town. He was right; it would have.

Arrived at the station, no talk or acting was of the slightest avail, and the judge next day held us each in $500 bail.

We raised that amount on jewelry, and, of course, "jumped" it and arrived at Boston together.

I was thoroughly disgusted with Lizzie, but she stuck to me like a leech, in spite of a dozen tricks that would have rid me of a detective.

At last I succeeded in getting away from her and happened to meet an all-round knight of the underworld known as "Frisco Farley." Together we worked the soda fountain trick, which was new then, and which I will explain in a later article.

In the course of the day we took in considerable profits, which had not been divided or even counted when we foolishly stepped into a jewelry store, merely to look at a new-fangled thief-proof showcase.

The first thing I knew, Farley was gone and I was arrested. It seems Farley had operated in that store a year ago, had been noticed and had escaped just in time. I was arrested as his accomplice.

On the way to the station what worried me most was the fact that I had in my pocket a ticket to New York. In Boston, for some reason, a ticket to New York is looked upon by the police as conclusive evidence of guilt.

I burst into tears and wailed and sobbed at the shame and humiliation of my arrest. By concealing the ticket in my handkerchief I managed to get it into my mouth as I wiped away my tears. Long before we reached the station house I had chewed up the small piece of pasteboard and swallowed it.

The story I told had only one weak spot. There was $400 more in my pocketbook than I thought, and this one discrepancy made them lock me up.

That night I was placed in a cell with an intoxicated woman. I was able to send out and get a bottle of whiskey, but not for myself. About midnight the woman woke up and was glad of a drink. I not only gave her one, but many, until she was in a stupor and made no protest when I changed clothes with her.

In those days, in Boston, it was usually the custom to let intoxicated persons sleep in a cell and then to put them out on the street in the morning without bringing them to court.

In the morning I pretended to be half sober and protested violently against being thrown out in the cold. But they pushed me out onto the sidewalk, much to my outward grief and inward joy.

I borrowed the price of a ticket to New York, leaving my money in the police station and my jewels at Springfield. Thus a week of hard, nerve-wrecking work netted me absolutely not one cent, but in reality the loss of my jewels, my time, and considerable money.

CHAPTER XII

GOOD DEEDS WHICH CRIMINALS DO AND WHICH SHOW THAT EVEN THE WORST THIEF IS NEVER WHOLLY BAD

A LIFE OF CRIME IS A LIFE OF HARD WORK, GREAT RISK, AND, COMPARA-tively speaking, small pay. Anyone who has followed these articles will agree at once that whatever the criminal gets out of his existence he pays very dearly for. Not only is he constantly running great physical dangers—the risk of being shot or otherwise injured and of being caught and imprisoned—but many of his most carefully planned criminal enterprises are doomed to failure and he has only his labor for his pains.

Quite frequently bank burglars devote as much as three or four months of hard labor in preparing for an important robbery and, in a large percentage of cases, they find that, after all their patience and industry, it is impossible for them to execute the robbery they have so carefully planned and all their work goes for naught. Sometimes, too, they are interrupted in their work and have to flee, leaving behind their kits of valuable tools. Watchmen's bullets are ever threatening their lives and prison walls constantly loom up before them.

In view of these facts one would imagine that the money which the professional criminal makes at such great risk and expense and with so much difficulty would have an enhanced value in his eyes. But this is not so. Not only is the professional criminal an inveterate gambler, as I have repeatedly pointed out, but the great majority of them are generous to a fault.

While this generosity is almost universal in the underworld, those unfamiliar with the workings of the criminal heart would give it very little credit for such impulses.

My experience in the underworld has thoroughly convinced me that no criminal is wholly bad. I know that beneath the rough exterior of many of the desperate criminals with whom I came in contact beat hearts that were tender. Today I shall relate some of the more striking incidents which come back to me and which illustrate some of the good qualities possessed by the notorious criminals with whom I associated.

I am reminded of an experience I had with Dan Nugent, the bank burglar. I may say incidentally that this man Nugent was absolutely fearless and would resort to any measure, however desperate, to accomplish his purpose. He was a man to be feared and it was dangerous to cross him. But that this criminal had some very excellent qualities will appear from the following incident, now told for the first time.

While in Kansas City I robbed a bank, securing some four thousand dollars. As I was leaving the bank—it was in the day time— I saw Nugent going in. Evidently he had planned to rob the bank himself. We did not speak.

Within a few minutes after my departure the robbery was discovered. The doors were at once closed and no one was allowed to leave without first undergoing the scrutiny of the detectives who had been summoned by telephone. Poor Dan was caught in the trap and his identity being established he was at once arrested on suspicion of having been implicated in the robbery, if not the actual perpetrator of it, although the only evidence against him was the fact of being on the premises.

Dan was kept in custody for some hours, but at length the police were compelled to let him go, being unable to strengthen their case against him.

Later that day I happened to run into him.

"Sophie," he said threateningly, "you owe me two thousand dollars!"

"How do you make that out!" I asked quite innocently, not knowing to what he was referring. I didn't know then that the robbery I had committed had been discovered and that Nugent had been arrested for it.

"SOPHIE, IF YOU DON'T HAND ME $2,000,
I'LL BLOW YOUR HEAD OFF"

"You got four thousand dollars in the bank this morning," he replied bitterly, "and I got arrested for it."

He seemed to be in a very ugly frame of mind and I knew he was not a man to be trifled with. I asked him to step into a cafe and talk it over. We entered the back room of a nearby saloon and Nugent ordered some drinks.

There were various persons seated at other tables in the place, but we attracted no particular attention. After the waiter had served us and left the room, Nugent took off his hat, held it across the table as though he were handing it to me, and beneath the shelter it afforded pointed a gun at me.

"Sophie, if you don't divide up on that job, I will blow your head off!" he threatened in a low voice.

I admit I was frightened, but I did not lose my head. Instead I began to cry copiously.

"Dan," I sobbed, "I declare by all I hold holy I didn't get any money in the bank this morning. I've just gotten out of jail and I'm dead broke. My poor children need lots of things I can't buy them. I wish I had got that money at the bank this morning, but I didn't. It must have been someone else who made a safe get-away, and I think it's pretty mean of you to treat me this way," and I began to cry more strenuously than ever.

Dan looked at me a moment searchingly and then, deciding that my grief was genuine, put up his gun.

"Don't cry, Sophie. I thought you got the money, and I wanted my bit, that's all. I'm sorry to have scared you. Forget it, old girl, and cheer up."

Nugent then asked me what the kids at home needed, and I told him everything I could think of. He took me by the arm and marched me into a dry goods store and made a number of purchases of the things he thought the children would want, and gave them to me, along with a little money for myself. We then parted, Nugent wishing me all kinds of luck and firmly believing in my fairy tale.

I really ought to have shared the money with Nugent—because I had stolen a march on him in robbing the bank before he got a chance, and he got into trouble through me. But I knew he had made a big haul in a bank a month previous, and I was practically without funds, so he could more easily afford the loss of the two thousand than I could. But, like most criminals, Nugent had a kind heart, and, when his finer nature was appealed to, he could not help being noble and generous.

As another illustration of the kindness of heart of some criminals, let me tell of a letter I received from a world-renowned criminal, whose name I will not now disclose. This unfortunate man is now serving a term in a foreign prison for a daring bank robbery in which he was caught through his anxiety to help a pal—although if he had thought only of himself he would have been free. I will quote from his letter to me and you will see the kindness that dwells in his big heart:

"My dear Pal:—Now, I want you to do me a little favor. Don't send me any money or presents at Christmas, but take the money that you would use on me, and go out and buy some turkeys and give them to some of the poor people who live around your place. It will make them feel good, and it will be a better way to use the money than to waste it by sending it over to me."

A man who can write such a thoughtful letter as the above and can sympathize with others in distress is not entirely a bad man, even though he is a convicted criminal. It is sad, indeed, to think that such a large hearted man should have to spend most of his days behind prison bars instead of being at some kind of labor where he could be of service to mankind and do all the decent things which his kindly thoughts of others would prompt him to do.

Not because I want to convey the impression that I am better than any of the other criminals whose exploits I am narrating, but, on the contrary, because the incident I am about to relate is typical of what notorious criminals are doing every day, I am going to tell of another experience in which I figured.

It was when I was in New York. One day, while loitering in a bank in the vicinity of Broadway and Chambers street, I observed a woman draw some money. She put it in a handkerchief and then placed the handkerchief in her pocket. I was in need of money pretty badly just then and decided to follow the woman and get the money.

After she came out of the bank I got close to her and had no trouble in taking out the handkerchief and the money. She was walking down toward the river front and, having started in that direction, too, I had to continue for a block or so in order not to excite suspicion by turning back. I walked a little behind the woman, and, when we reached the middle of the block, she stopped and spoke to me:

"I beg your pardon, madame, but can you tell me where the French line steamboats dock?"

I directed her to the proper place and we got into conversation. She told me that she was going home to her mother in France in order to die there. She had been given up by the doctors here as an incurable consumptive and had sold all her goods for a few hundred dollars with which she was to pay her fare and give the rest to her mother. I became interested in this, for it seemed to me that I had robbed a woman in distress of her last dollar, and that was something I did not like to do.

I asked her if she had money besides the amount she drew out of the bank (she had told me of taking the money from the bank), and she said that was all she had in the world. I could not think of keeping her money after that, because, when the poor woman reached the ticket office and found her money gone and her trip abroad impossible, she would probably have died of the shock. So I determined to put the money back in the poor French woman's pocket. I walked along with her to the ticket office and, while she was talking to the agent, I slipped the money back in her pocket. She bought her ticket and went aboard the boat and I felt pleased that I had not kept the money.

That evening I told some of my criminal friends of the transaction, and several of them seemed disgusted with me because I had not put in some money of my own along with the small mite the woman had so that she would be cheered up a bit. They thought it mean of me not to do more than I did to help along a woman so unfortunate as this sick woman.

On several other occasions I voluntarily returned stolen money to people when I found out that they were more in need of it than myself. I stole a satchel from a woman in a bank once and it contained a few hundred dollars. The next day I discovered in the paper that the woman was blind and I was referred to as the meanest kind of a thief. When I learned this I hastened to return the money to the unfortunate woman. I never could sleep easy if I thought that any really deserving person suffered from my thieving. I tried to confine my work to people who could afford to lose their money and would soon forget the affair. A very poor person who loses the savings of a lifetime never gets over the shock of his or her loss and it causes real suffering. It didn't worry me any to make people feel resentful and indignant, but I could not bear the thought of making anybody unhappy.

I was in Paris many years ago and stopping at one of the most fashionable hotels in the city. Mrs. Lorillard, the society woman, was occupying rooms adjoining mine, and I was trying to get her jewelry. She always carried a great amount of jewelry with her, and I knew the prize was a good one. She had two maids with her, one of whom had to keep watch over two satchels in which the jewelry was secreted.

The maids were honest girls and we could not do any business through them, but we followed the party from place to place expecting that some time the girl would forget to take proper care of her satchels, and then our opportunity to steal them would arrive. A few days after Mrs. Lorillard had settled at this hotel she attended some reception in Paris and, of course, her jewelry bags had to be taken from the hotel safe, where they had been placed for safety.

Mrs. Lorillard picked out the particular pieces of jewelry she wanted to wear at the reception and closed up the two bags, turning them over to the maid to place in the safe. The maid came out of the apartment with the two bags, and I met her in the hall and began to ask her some trivial question. She stopped to talk with me and laid down the bags. While I kept her engaged in conversation a comrade of mine crept up, substituted another bag for one of the jewelry receptacles, and skipped off. I continued to talk a little longer and then the girl and I parted, she going downstairs to the safe with the two bags, not suspecting that I had deliberately held her in conversation while my friend had taken one of the precious bags.

My associate went to another hotel and concealed the jewelry, while I stayed there in my room, not wishing to attract attention by leaving at such a critical time, for, after the robbery was discovered, if it had been found that I had left at the same time it would have been natural for suspicion to be directed at me.

The following day, when the bags were sent for in order for Mrs. Lorillard to put back the jewels she had worn at the reception, it was found that one of the bags was missing and there was great excitement. Detectives by the score were sent for and the whole hotel was searched top and bottom for a clue.

That evening, after I had retired, I heard a woman sobbing in the adjoining room, and, as the sobs continued for some time, I knocked and asked if I could be of assistance to her. She opened the door and invited me into her room. It was Mrs. Lorillard. She told me of the robbery and said that it was not the jewelry she worried about but the loss of a picture of her dead child which was very dear to her. She thought more of the picture than the jewels and her grief over its disappearance was pathetic. I consoled her as best I could, and told her I had had some experience as a detective and thought I could secure the return of the picture without any trouble, especially as it was not valuable to the thieves. The following day I took back the picture to the woman and she was overjoyed at its return. After remaining in the hotel long enough not to excite suspicion by my departure, I left to meet my pals and divide the proceeds of the job. The jewels we had taken were the best in the Lorillard collection, and each one of the party made a good profit on the transaction. A number of years after this event Mrs. Lorillard committed suicide, which was induced by a spell of melancholy, brought on probably by thoughts of her dead boy, whom she dearly loved.

I have already mentioned how Langdon W. Moore, the notorious bank burglar, whose activities in New England made him more feared throughout that section than any other criminal who ever operated, once frustrated an attempt to rob a bank at Francetown, New Hampshire, after having consented to participate in it, because the bank was located near his own birthplace and he did not feel like robbing his parents' old neighbors.

This man Langdon, like many other criminals of the same caliber, made it a rule of his life never to use violence. Frequently he abandoned a contemplated criminal enterprise upon which he had spent months of hard work because he found that he could not carry out his original plan without injuring a watchman or other person.

Of course, when hard pressed it was sometimes necessary for Langdon to fight his way to liberty, but in such cases he always made reparation to the injured man as far as lay in his power. On one occasion, when he had fractured the skull of an officer who had sought to capture him, he caused $2,500 in cash to be sent to the injured man.

Other criminals frequently exhibit similar noble qualities.

Loyalty to his comrades is another trait found in almost every professional criminal. "Honor among thieves" is a phrase commonly used, but few realize upon what a strong foundation it rests. I know of innumerable instances where criminals risked their own liberty and even their lives in order to assist a comrade in danger.

Mark Shinburn, the noted bank burglar, once displayed bravery and loyalty of a character which is seldom excelled even on the battlefield. He had participated with Eddie Quinn and a third bank burglar in the robbery of a Western bank. Just as the three were leaving the bank the watchman appeared upon the scene. There was nothing to do but run. The watchman opened fire. Quinn dropped. Without a moment's hesitation Shinburn stopped in his flight, although the watchman was close upon them, and, lifting his fallen comrade to his broad shoulders, continued his flight at reduced speed.

Shinburn was a very powerful fellow and even with his wounded comrade on his shoulders he was able to outrun the watchman. He soon caught up with the third man of the party and they made for the woods. When they lowered Quinn to the ground they found that he was dying. The burglar had only a few minutes to live. Quinn was conscious and begged his comrades to get a priest to administer the last rites, realizing that his end was near.

The two men with him knew it was impossible to get a priest, but they wanted to make the last moments of Quinn's life as happy as possible. To leave the woods at this time, however, was to invite capture, for the watchman had undoubtedly aroused the neighborhood and the woods would naturally be the first place searched for the fugitives. Nevertheless Shinburn decided to take a chance and left the dying man to comply with his last wish. He knew that it would be almost impossible to get a priest, but he broke into a furnishing store on the outskirts of the woods and went back to his dying comrade wearing a costume very much like that of a priest.

The approaching hand of death had dimmed the dying burglar's sight and he had no suspicion that the "priest" was his big-hearted comrade. In a slow, solemn tone Shinburn spoke words of encouragement to his dying friend, and the unfortunate man passed away, comforted by what he thought were the sacred words of a priest.

But instances of noble deeds among criminals whose souls are generally believed to be wholly black might be narrated without end. These men and women who declare war against society only to find that crime does not pay are not without their redeeming qualities.

Their evil deeds are published far and wide, but the good that they do seldom comes to light.

ABOUT COMBUSTION BOOKS

Combustion books is a collectively-run publisher of dangerous fiction. We specialize in genre stories that confront, subvert, or rudely ignore the dominant paradigm and we're not afraid to get our hands dirty or our houses raided by the government. How many fiction publishers can promise you that?

Rejecting the dominant paradigm doesn't end with the stories we tell. We operate without bosses and we pay ourselves and our authors outright for work in order to keep us from getting mired in the world of profit-driven publishing.

One of our goals is to break down the hierarchy of the publishing world and develop relationships with our authors and audience that go beyond those offered by a traditional press.

We're open to manuscript submissions and delight in working with new and un-agented authors. We are primarily interested in novel-length (40,000+ words) genre fiction of a radical bent. Genres we're seeking include SF, Fantasy, Horror, Steampunk, Mystery, and New Weird.

Please attach completed manuscripts for consideration, in .rtf, .doc, .odt, or .docx format, to an email directed to SUBMISSIONS@COMBUSTIONBOOKS.ORG. We will respond within 30 days of receiving your submission. Please do not send multiple manuscripts: send only your best work. If you have written a series, send only the first in the series.

CPSIA information can be obtained at www.ICGtesting.com
Printed in the USA
BVOW04s0146311013

335114BV00004B/25/P